52692

COLLEGE LIBRARY

**Please return this book by the date stamped below
- if recalled, the loan is reduced to 10 days**

Fines are payable for late return

SHAKESPEARE AND THE SOLITARY MAN

SHAKESPEARE AND
THE SOLITARY MAN

JANETTE DILLON

First published 1981 by
THE MACMILLAN PRESS LTD
London and Basingstoke
Companies and representatives
throughout the world

Printed in Hong Kong

British Library Cataloguing in Publication Data

Dillon, Janette
  Shakespeare and the solitary man
    1. Shakespeare, William – Criticism and
  interpretation
    2. Solitude in literature
  I. Title
  822.3'3   PR3069.S

ISBN 0-333-27468-7

For Malcolm

Contents

Acknowledgements

The author and publishers wish to thank the editors of *JEGP* for permission to reproduce material which has already appeared in that journal in a somewhat different form.

The quotations from Shakespeare's plays are taken from *The Complete Works of William Shakespeare*, edited by Peter Alexander, published by William Collins Sons & Co. Ltd.

I should also like to thank the following people: Anne Barton, who encouraged me from the start and who has remained a constant influence towards both breadth and order in the book; Penry Williams, who gave me the benefit of his wide-ranging knowledge of the history of the period; Andrew Gurr, who kindly read an early draft and who has improved the book in many ways by his attention to detail and his ability always to suggest new perspectives; Katherine Duncan-Jones, who helped to kindle my interest in Elizabethan literature and consistently offered advice and support; Barrie Bullen, who willingly read the whole typescript and made suggestions for improvement; and Roger Holdsworth, who gave his time and attention so generously to the discussion of even the smallest detail, and whose close knowledge of Elizabethan and Jacobean drama saved me from many errors. For errors that remain I can have no-one but myself to blame.

November, 1979.   J.D.

List of Abbreviations

CritQ	*Critical Quarterly*
EA	*Etudes Anglaises*
EETS	Early English Text Society
EIC	*Essays in Criticism*
JEGP	*Journal of English and Germanic Philology*
JHI	*Journal of the History of Ideas*
MLR	*Modern Language Review*
MP	*Modern Philology*
PMLA: Publications of the Modern Language Association of America	
PQ	*Philological Quarterly*
SF&R	Scholars' Facsimiles and Reprints
ShS	*Shakespeare Survey*
SQ	*Shakespeare Quarterly*
TSIL	*Texas Studies in Literature and Language*

Titles of Shakespeare's plays are abbreviated in accordance with the practice now adopted by leading Shakespeare journals, as set out in *PMLA*, 85 (1970), 322.

Note on the Text

Quotations from Shakespeare, unless otherwise stated, are taken from Peter Alexander's edition of *The Complete Works* (1951). The dating of Shakespeare's plays follows the Riverside chronology. I have retained the original spelling and punctuation in the titles of, and quotations from, unedited early texts, except to modernise obsolete letters and i/j and u/v spelling forms. Typographical conventions have also been revised to conform with modern practice and obvious misprints silently corrected where necessary.

Introduction

Consideration of the solitary in Shakespeare must begin with the most uncompromising and widely quoted affirmations of self-sufficiency in the whole canon:

I am myself alone   (*3H6*, v. vi. 78–83)

Richard loves Richard; that is, I am I.   (*R3*, v. iii. 183)

These are the statements of Richard III, and they are most often labelled by modern critics as assertions of 'individualism'. The Elizabethans, however, had no such term, and they would have described Richard's self-enclosed inwardness, his devotion to self at the expense of society, as well as his physical isolation, as 'solitariness', a quality which they habitually classified as being of time, place or mind.[1] Any characteristic which indicated interest in the self and the inner world, or which implied a morality that valued the self above the common good might be described as 'solitariness'. Self-love, detachment, a contemplative bent, a sense of individual superiority, a cultivation of distinctiveness, any anti-social or even simply asocial behaviour, might be seen by the Elizabethans as a form of solitude. Any behaviour or set of values which seemed to define the individual from within, without relation to society, or in opposition to society, was a statement of isolation, a separation of the self from the wider human context.[2]

Richard's statements of isolation are usually seen as self-evident pointers to Shakespeare's disapproval of Richard; and critics frequently take these as indicating Shakespeare's general disapproval of individualism, a disapproval which is supposed to distinguish him from his contemporaries. Ian Jack, comparing Shakespeare with Webster, writes:

It is consonant with Webster's unbalanced outlook that the distinguishing mark of his Machiavellian 'heroes' is their individualism. In Shakespeare individualism is an infallible mark of villainy:

Richard loves Richard; that is, I am I.

Like Richard III, Iago and Edmund in Shakespeare, Lodovico, the Cardinal, Bosola and Flamineo are all individualists, and all villains.[3]

L. C. Knights writes of Shakespeare:

... the distrust that he shows, from first to last, for individualism—for the attitude expressed in Richard of Gloucester's 'I am myself alone'—is based on a sure grasp of the self-mutilation inherent in egotism and isolation, of the inevitable denaturing effect of an attitude that wilfully blinds itself to the fact that personal life only has its being in relationship: Macbeth as tyrant inevitably 'keeps alone'.[4]

But when Richard's statements are transformed into the 'I am that I am' of Sonnet 121 or Hamlet's cherishing of 'the heart of my mystery' (III. ii. 356–7), is it still possible to see individualism as 'an infallible mark of villainy'? M. C. Bradbrook cites Richard's statements of self-definition as symptomatic of his villainy, but does so in order to draw attention to a change in Shakespeare's attitude with *Hamlet*, rather than to use Richard as representative of an attitude retained 'from first to last':

Hamlet, the solitary muser, was an *innovation*; it is on the whole not till the seventeenth century that praise of solitude becomes a general thing. Only villains, like Lorenzo and Richard III, will say, 'I'll trust myself: myself shall be my friend' 'I am myself alone' or 'Richard loves Richard: that is, I am I'.[5]

She makes the point that Shakespeare lived at a time when attitudes to solitude were changing: whereas in the sixteenth century it was the mark of villains, in the seventeenth century it was generally praised.

Hamlet was not, however, an innovation entirely alien and unprepared for. He was the first hero whose solitariness had been presented so fully, so sympathetically, and so much from within; but the more equivocal and hesitant beginnings of a preference for solitude had been evident in England from about 1570, and from much earlier in Europe. Nor did *Hamlet* mark the end of equivocation. Solitude did not become automatically admirable or even acceptable at the turn of the century, and even *Hamlet* does not offer solitude as a focus for unreserved admiration. Hamlet, 'the solitary muser', is also lonely.

The word 'solitariness' (the Elizabethans rarely used 'solitude') became conspicuously prevalent, according to the OED, between about 1570 and 1700, and it is the crucial period of transition, from about 1570 to 1630, with which this book is primarily concerned. This is the period in which the shifting balance between individual and social concerns provokes the most violent controversy, the most extreme statements and the most blatant self-contradiction. It is a time characterised by inconsistency, hesitation, qualification and equivocation, by irreconcilable statements of opposing absolutes rather than by measured certainty. The pressure on traditional ideas is revealed at this stage more by the urgency of the debate than by the conclusions reached. Impassioned defence of the old social ideals suggests as strongly as open attack the challenging of conventional attitudes.

The general drift in the late sixteenth century was away from the medieval idealisation of the bonds between men towards an increased reverence for the individual enclosed in his inner world, in isolation from other men. Men were ceasing to judge the individual by how well he fulfilled his appointed place in society and how much he contributed to the collective good, and were beginning to judge him instead as a self-contained and autonomous unit. The inner world of the mind came to assume greater importance, the pleasures of solitude and introspection began to usurp the sense of community, and participation in society was increasingly regarded as a duty conflicting with the individual desire for privacy. Arguments in favour of solitude in the sixteenth century were framed largely in terms of pleasure and personal choice, while arguments in defence of an active social life were framed in moral terms. There was little attempt either to extol the pleasures of civil life or to justify solitude in moral terms until well into the seventeenth century.

During this period of transition, when solitude was approved in terms of its attractiveness and condemned in terms of moral duty, there arose a cult of solitude which seems to have reached a peak in the 1590s. Arguments from the principle of individual will can easily develop into a cult, which sets up the individual in opposition to the established standards of the time. Once the standards of the cult become part of the establishment, the cult itself necessarily ceases, since the position it championed has ceased to be that of an advanced minority. Solitude, then, can only be said to have been a cult as long as those who cultivated it were seen as affected and morally reprehensible. Once solitude became morally respectable, after about the first quarter of the seventeenth century, it ceased to be a cult and became an altogether more lukewarm version of its former self, a state of monied leisure and moral self-satisfaction rather than a flagrant challenge to social values. Even the shift in vocabulary towards more moderate words than 'solitariness' ('recess', 'secess', 'retirement' and so on) indicates a modification in the ideal itself.[6]

After its brief flirtation with secularism and amorality, the ideal solitude became a religious and moral state in the later seventeenth century, as it had been in the Middle Ages for religious hermits. John Aubrey even lamented the loss of monasteries as refuges for contemplative men.[7] There were two main differences between the medieval and the seventeenth-century contemplative ideals: first, the medieval contemplative's solitude was total or almost total, whereas the seventeenth-century contemplative was scarcely solitary at all in any physical sense; and second, the medieval contemplative was exceptional among his contemporaries and could be supported in his vocation only because most men chose the active life of full social participation, whereas the seventeenth-century pursuit of leisured contemplation was widespread and symptomatic of a general absence of public-spiritedness or faith in a social ideal.

Shakespeare's working life falls approximately in the middle of the period of transition when solitude was at its most fashionable, its most daringly attractive and its most morally uncertain. It is to be expected, then, that the turmoil of ideas on this subject around him should be reflected in his work and should have contributed to the formation of his own attitudes. I have tried to show in this book the importance of the contemporary preoccupation with solitude to Shakespeare and, through a study of the changing status of the solitary figure in his work, to indicate the development of his attitudes in relation to those of his contemporaries. Such a study is necessarily selective: consideration of all the works of Shakespeare which have some bearing on his attitude to solitude is beyond the range of any one book. I have tried instead to cover a representative range as regards both date and genre so as to suggest Shakespeare's continuing preoccupation with the subject as well as the changes in his responses to it. The chapters are arranged chronologically, but no importance attaches to the exact dating for the purposes of the argument. It does not matter, for instance, whether the Sonnets were written largely before or after *Richard II*, or in what order the plays from *King Lear* to *Timon of Athens* were written; the only distinction that needs to be made here is between the first two as early and the last group as late.

Broadly, I argue, with Professor Bradbrook, for an enlarging of Shakespeare's sympathy for the solitary after *Richard III*, which reaches a climax in *Hamlet*, but subsides again in the later plays.[8] This enlargement of sympathy does not, however, represent a change in moral judgement, but rather a change in emphasis, whereby the moral judgement takes second place to the understanding and sympathy with which the character is presented. Shakespeare never allows the audience to forget the loss that the solitary experiences by cutting himself off from his fellow men. Hamlet's solitude is not held up as an ideal but as a cruel necessity in a corrupt society. Polonius's advice to Laertes:

This above all—to thine own self be true,
And it must follow, as the night the day,
Thou canst not then be false to any man (I. iii. 78–80)

is a statement which is only true in an ideal society. Hamlet finds that in order to be true to himself he has to play false in society, and that is an indictment of the society in which he finds himself rather than of him. Shakespeare is not showing in *Hamlet* that the morality of being true to oneself is a higher one than the morality of being true to society; he is depicting a situation where the individual is faced not with a society which embodies ideal reciprocity between its members but with one that is corrupted and in which the most sacred of the social bonds have been violated. Recognising this with regret, the individual is then forced to choose between two sets of values which ideally should mutually enhance one another, and chooses self. But he chooses reluctantly, and there is no suggestion that such division between the inward and the social self is desirable. There is no doubt that the ideal would be integrity of being, where the private and the public selves were one and the individual contributed to and found fulfilment in society.

The fact that Shakespeare wrote *Hamlet* at all indicates that the debate on the relative values of society and the solitary preoccupied him, and in this preoccupation he is at one with his times; but the emphasis of the play, and more clearly of other plays, points to an ideal of reciprocity between the individual and society, of a mutual bond which made self-fulfilment inherent in and inseparable from society, and this ideal was inherited from medieval writers. Those plays of Shakespeare's which place the solitary individual at their centre are inevitably tragedies, and tragedies which arise directly, if not exclusively, out of that initial severance of self from society. The changing perspective and emphasis of Shakespeare's writing up to *Hamlet* at the turn of the century follow the general contemporary trend towards increased interest in the inner world of the self in isolation, but his moral judgements do not. His judgement is in line with the contemporary movement only in that he ceases to present the solitary as a moral degenerate; he does not follow the continuation of that movement to the point of celebrating the individual who has freed himself from all external bonds and created his own autonomous morality. Such an individual remains unfulfilled, the object not of unqualified celebration, but of admiration mingled with pity.

Part One

I Approaches to Solitude before Shakespeare

A brief survey of the areas of classical literature which were influential in shaping the attitudes to solitude in sixteenth- and seventeenth-century England is a necessary prologue to discussion of the later period. Indeed, it is interesting to note that the movement of ideas in Renaissance England followed a similar pattern to movements illustrated in Greek and Roman literature: that is, from idealisation of the state and the individual's duty to the common good to the expression of a desire for solitude and an emphasis on the private, inner world of the individual.

Plato and Aristotle in Greece and Cicero in Rome were the main exponents of the ideal of the city-state, and of these Plato was the least familiar in Renaissance England. These three were united in their insistence that the individual's first duty was to the state. Even Plato, who sympathised most with the individual longing for solitude, insisted that a philosopher must leave his solitary contemplations if called upon to participate in the government of the state.[1] Aristotle and Cicero, although they acknowledged the value of the contemplative life, shared a deep revulsion from the idea of solitude. Solitude, according to Aristotle, was 'a very terrible thing, because the whole of life and voluntary association is with friends',[2] and Cicero believed that if a wise man studied in a solitude 'so complete that he could never see a human being, he would die'.[3]

The most difficult paradox arising out of this horror of solitude was the need to reconcile it with the acknowledged ideal of self-sufficiency. Aristotle stated flatly that 'the final cause and end of a thing is the best, and to be self-sufficing is the end and the best'[4] but felt forced elsewhere to extend the definition of self in order to avoid seeming to recommend solitude: 'The term self-sufficient, however, we employ with reference not to oneself alone, living a life of

3

isolation, but also to one's parents and children and wife, and one's friends and fellow citizens in general since man is by nature a social being.'[5] He then went on to acknowledge the potential absurdity of extending this qualification. Throughout his writing he reaffirmed the undesirability of solitude and the necessity for full participation in the state. His most famous denunciation of the solitary occurs in the *Politics*:

> And he who by nature and not by mere accident is without a state, is either a bad man or above humanity; he is like the 'Tribeless, lawless, heartless one', whom Homer denounces— the natural outcast is forthwith a lover of war; he may be compared to an isolated piece at draughts . . . he who is unable to live in society, or who has no need because he is sufficient for himself, must be either a beast or a god: he is no part of a state.[6]

The last part of this pronouncement was especially widely quoted and alluded to throughout the sixteenth century.

The reaction of the Stoics against the Athenian ideal of public life began shortly after Aristotle's death, although to some extent the Stoics simply highlighted a contradiction already inherent in Aristotle's work between the ideals of self-sufficiency and the contemplative life on the one hand and the duty to the state and hatred of solitude on the other. It was through the work of a much later writer, Seneca, that Stoic thought exerted its influence on Elizabethan England, and the conflict between different ideals is a conspicuous element in his work. Participation in the state, an ideal which united pleasure with duty for Aristotle, became more clearly a duty alone in Seneca, one which conflicted with the personal desire for solitude in which to cultivate the inner life. What seems self-contradiction in Seneca is in fact a separation between public and private ideals; and in his allotting of two different terminologies, of morality and pleasure, to the subjects of the civil and the solitary lives respectively, Seneca anticipated Petrarch and later English writers.

These later writers, however, distorted Seneca as they did Aristotle. From Aristotle they extracted the praise of social life and from Seneca the praise of the solitary and introspective life, without acknowledging the qualifications and contradictions in either. But both those who praised and those who denounced solitude used the same criterion as justification for their respective standpoints:

nature. While the social ideal could refer to Aristotle's definition of man as 'by nature a social being' for its authority, the pursuit of solitude could be validated with reference to the recommendation of both Cicero and Seneca, that a man should follow his own nature. Cicero, who never intended this advice to be read as an invitation to individual autonomy, uses the word 'nature' in two very different ways in this context, illustrating the ambiguity inherent in the word. The proviso that 'we must so act as not to oppose the universal laws of human nature' firmly establishes the limits within which his advice to follow one's individual nature should be read.[7] The context thus attempts to reconcile the ideals of the individual and the collective good, not to set up the first in opposition to the second.

The word 'nature' retained its ambiguity, and Elizabethan writers, though continuing to exploit this ambiguity in debating the respective claims of particular nature and social obligation, complained of its lack of definition. John Donne, for example, exclaims irritably in *Biathanatos* (1646): 'This terme the law of Nature, is so variously and unconstantly deliver'd, as I confesse I read it a hundred times before I understand it once, or can conclude it to signifie that which the author should at that time meane,'[8] thereby admitting that its usage is almost wholly subjective and relative. This absence of any agreement about the meaning of 'nature' made for particular difficulty surrounding the concept of the 'law of nature' which Donne mentions, since the collective principle contained in the word 'law' is at odds with the flexibility of the word 'nature', which should define the principle. The law of nature is a concept which balances individual and social concerns, the inner and the collective moral orders. It seeks to reconcile individual freedom and obedience to collectively acknowledged morality, but in seeking the point of intersection between extremes it understandably becomes open to unbalanced interpretation and abuse, and is easily distorted to become the war-cry of one or the other extreme.

'Nature' in quite a different sense was at the centre of a completely separate classical tradition which was very influential on the later literature of solitude: the lyrical tradition of the happy husbandman. The praise of individual freedom, simplicity, innocence and relative isolation associated with the country life in this poetry, and particularly in the poetry of Virgil and Horace, inspired English poets from Wyatt to the Cavalier poets and after. This line of influence has been fully discussed elsewhere,[9] and it is sufficient here simply to note its importance in emphasising the moral superiority of the retired life. By contrast with Aristotle's presentation of duty and desire coinciding in the civil life, or Seneca's division of duty from desire in recommending the social and the solitary lives respectively, the lyrical tradition praises the retired life as both more desirable than and morally superior to the civil life.

Classical pastoral and satire were also important, but rather specialised, influences on Renaissance attitudes to the withdrawal from society, which I shall not attempt to discuss here, particularly since these genres, if not their classical origins, will be discussed in Chapter 7. The last important area of influence, which can only be sketched here, is the concept of the hero, as formed jointly by Greek and Roman history, epic and drama, particularly tragedy. The classical hero cannot be described in the way that lyrics in praise of solitude can, since obviously there is no one fixed set of values to which every hero corresponds. Nevertheless, it is important to recognise the tendency of these three genres to focus on a single individual, to present the action and ideas through a central 'hero', however he is defined. Solitude may not be explicitly praised in any of these genres; it may on the contrary be condemned or pitied, if it is presented at all. But simply the singling out of one man, a leader who stands apart from his fellows, or a man of exceptional qualities, was easily adapted by the Elizabethans into the ardent individualism and defiant isolation which characterises so many of their heroes.

The protagonists of Plutarch's histories are rarely solitary by nature (though there are exceptions, like Coriolanus), but they do exist on a level apart from those who surround them and our impression of public events is partly determined by the way in which they can be related to the private experience of these exceptional individuals.[10] Similarly the epic heroes are scarcely solitary, but they are the vehicles through which events of far-reaching social significance are mediated.

Reuben Brower has demonstrated how the Elizabethans were specifically attracted by any elements of solitariness in these heroes, particularly in Aeneas. Their preference for Virgil over Homer is, he argues, a preference for a private, meditative hero over one revealed wholly by his actions. Chapman's translation of Homer shows the characteristic distortion of the age in its tendency to play down feats of physical heroism and to insert more meditation.[11]

Greek tragedy seems to have had little effect on English

Renaissance drama,[12] and it was the plays of Seneca that did most to form the Elizabethan tragic hero. Seneca's heroes were more isolated, as the protagonists of tragedy, than the heroes of history and epic, and can be distinguished from epic heroes by their 'immense sense of self'.[13] Much more of the action is internal in tragedy than in the other two genres, and the tragic hero is clearly set apart from his society in a spiritual, if not a physical, isolation.

Taken together, then, history, epic and tragedy can be seen to exhibit a common tendency to glorify the individual. While they do not actually praise withdrawal from society or recommend that the individual consider himself before his social obligations, they do focus on exceptional and superior individuals, set apart from society by their very natures, and by implication set a higher value on the individual's cultivation of heroic quality in himself than on his participation in society. Their emphasis is on the aspiration towards self-sufficiency and self-perfection rather than on the individual's duty to the whole in which he is a mere part.

MEDIEVAL

From the Anglo-Saxon writers to Malory in the fifteenth century the general feeling expressed towards the solitary was primarily one of pity. The exile, the rootless man cut off from the bonds and duties of society, represented not freedom and self-sufficiency, but incompleteness and meaninglessness. The solitary Wanderer, in the Anglo-Saxon lyric of that name, feels himself to be a fragment, a part severed from his bonds with the community as a whole, yearning for what he feels to be the natural bonds of service, fellowship and kinship. In Malory the value placed on fellowship is even higher than on sexual love: Arthur is tormented more by the breaking of the Round Table fellowship than by the loss of Gwenyvere, and Launcelot, having taken Gwenyvere to Joyous Garde to save her life, is willing to return her to Arthur if by so doing he can prevent the destruction of the fellowship in civil war. Perhaps the most emotive word in Malory is 'togydirs' (together), for by the fifteenth century the word was already charged with nostalgia for a bygone age which seemed, at least to Malory, characterised by its love of the 'common weal' above the individual good.

Most writers before 1500, and many after that date, define the individual not from within, in isolation from society, but as a part in a greater whole, meaningful only in context. The ideal therefore is not, as in classical times, self-sufficiency, but mutual support, and individual virtue is measured by its contribution to the common good. St Thomas Aquinas quotes Augustine as his authority in insisting on the necessity for the individual to mould himself in accordance with principles of community:

> The goodness of any part is considered in comparison with the whole; hence Augustine says (*Conf.* iii) that *unseemly is the part that harmonizes not with the whole.* Since then every man is a part of the state, it is impossible that a man be good, unless he be well proportionate to the common good: nor can the whole be well consistent unless its parts be proportionate to it.[14]

For Aquinas the perfect state and the perfect individual are complementary, not contradictory ends: the individual is instrumental in the achievement of the common good, and the ideal community is instrumental in helping the individual to attain a virtuous life. The community is not, however, the only means whereby the individual can attain such virtue. Man's first duty is to God, and the social life is only the commonest way of fulfilling this duty. In a few cases, God inspires the individual to seek Him through the solitary life of contemplation. Aquinas's Commentary on Aristotle's *Politics* glosses Aristotle's assertion that the solitary is either a beast or a god in order to accommodate the voluntary solitude of religious contemplatives:

> If any man should be such that he is not a political being by nature, he is either wicked—as when this happens through the corruption of human nature—or he is better than man—in that he has a nature more perfect than that of other men in general, so that he is able to be sufficient to himself without the society of men, as were John the Baptist and St Anthony the hermit.[15]

The praise of self-sufficiency here differs from the classical praise of self-sufficiency in that it is recognised as a solitary state and as an ideal appropriate only in exceptional cases and only with religious motivation. Praise of solitude in the Middle Ages, then, is found only in religious writings. Solitude in a secular context is pitied as the manifestation of some tormented state, such as love, madness, or grief; the notion of unmotivated solitude, delighted in for its own sake, simply does not occur.

Religious writers vary in the intensity of the solitude they recommend, and many advocate the mixed life in place of either absolute, active or contemplative.[16] Distinctions are made too between internal and external solitude. Walter Hilton, for example, sees internal solitude as the real end of the contemplative (see p. xi n. 1 above) and advises him that physical solitude ('onlyness') and company ('communing') are equally valid ways of achieving spiritual detachment from the world.[17] But most are less open-minded, and assume physical isolation in some degree to be essential for the contemplative life. Abelard denounces monks for transforming monasteries, founded to foster the complete isolation of the individual monk, into small communities.[18] *Ancrene Wisse* lists eight reasons for keeping alone, and quotes innumerable passages of Scripture to reinforce the point.[19]

The ambiguity of Scripture, however, produced constant wrangling over the relative merits of solitude and society until the end of the seventeenth century. Richard Rolle in the fourteenth century, for example, berates those who quote the warning from Ecclesiastes, 'wo unto him that is alone' (4:10),[20] in order to condemn religious enclosure. They have, he insists, misconstrued the texts: 'they do not define "alone" as being "without God", but understand it to mean "without company".'[21] The solitude of Adam before the creation of Eve and God's statement of his reason for creating Eve: 'It is not good that the man should be himself alone' (Gen. 2:18) were particularly familiar authorities interpreted to justify both solitude and society.

Medieval writers formulated ideals of opposing extremity: the ideal of an active life involving full participation, uniting duty and desire in the twin conception of contribution to and fulfilment from society; and the ideal of a contemplative life involving complete withdrawal from society, both physical and spiritual, total dedication to God without the distractions of worldly commitments. The sixteenth century inherited the debate on solitude at a time when the active and contemplative ideals were at their most absolute and uncompromising.

EARLY SIXTEENTH CENTURY

The sixteenth century marked the beginning of a more practical idealism. It inherited from medieval writers the ideal of a perfect commonwealth in which the individual might achieve a virtuous life, but began to emphasise political reform more strongly than moral reform as a means of achieving this end.[22] Sixteenth-century writers continued to acknowledge the same moral absolutes as before, but within this framework they gave more consideration to the relativity of the individual commonwealth to its time and place and to the activities of particular men, and less to man's fallen nature and God's inscrutable plan. Though not irreligious, their approach was increasingly secular, and a fashion for political literature began to usurp the pre-eminence of religious and moral writings. Gabriel Harvey, writing to Spenser in the 1570s, draws attention simultaneously to the fashion for political literature and to the fact that English fashion had its source in European fashion at this time: 'You can not stepp into a schollars studye but (ten to on) you shall litely finde open ether Bodin de Republica or Le Royes Exposition uppon Aristotles Politiques or sum other like French or Italian Politique Discourses'.[23]

The sixteenth-century ideal of the 'veray and true common-weal'[24] remained medieval in many respects. The individual was still encouraged to see himself as contributing to a whole greater than himself and to consider his duty to the state before his individual good. In Thomas Starkey's words, 'Overmuch regard of private and particular weal ever destroyeth the common, as mean and convenient regard thereof maintaineth the same.'[25] Society was still seen as natural to man in general rather than considered in relation to the nature of each individual man. Without society, writes Sir Thomas Elyot, 'mannes lyfe is unpleasaunt and full of anguisshe'.[26] Starkey even redefines the law of nature as the social impulse: 'This inclination and rule of living . . . is called . . . the law of nature, which, though all men follow not, yet all men approve.'[27]

The main difference between medieval and early sixteenth-century attitudes was the virtual disappearance of the exception to the rule, contemplative withdrawal. Withdrawal from the community was condemned whatever the motivations, and the dissolution of the monasteries during this period emphasises the fervour of that condemnation. Starkey presents the contemplative life not as a valid alternative to, but as an escape from, the difficulties of an active life, ridiculing the man who 'runneth into a religious house, there as in a haven quietly to rest, without so much trouble and disquietness'.[28] Every man without exception, according to Archbishop Laud, 'must live in the body of the Commonwealth and in the body of the Church'.[29]

Yet the discrediting of the contemplative ideal was not so uncontested as such definitive statements suggest. Evidence of a conflict between the continuing impulse towards religious enclosure and the public-spiritedness which demanded full participation in civil life can be seen in the life and writings of Sir Thomas More. More long considered the possibility of ordination, and spent four years in religious contemplation before he finally chose the law as his profession. Even after this he continued to display an asceticism reminiscent of medieval solitaries and wore a hair-shirt under his clothes. It is perhaps symptomatic of More's own uncertainty that his *Utopia* (1516) has been read both as a commendation and as a condemnation of the monastic life.

The attraction of the contemplative life in the sixteenth century is widely represented by a secularised and less absolute type of solitary than the medieval hermit: the scholar. The scholar's withdrawal is only relative, and only justified by his combination of knowledge with action. Public usefulness is the criterion by which private pleasure is judged in this period. 'No man is born for himself alone' is an obsessively recurring dictum in diatribes against the solitude or self-love, and expresses an ethos which has both classical and Biblical authority.

Conflict between a personal impulse towards privacy and a sense of duty towards society can be seen in the sixteenth-century debate on the problem of whether or not the scholar should use his learning for the common good by offering his counsel at court. The choice was admittedly not so extreme for the sixteenth-century scholar as it had been for the medieval hermit: it was a choice not between civil life and total solitude, but between active participation in affairs of state and a relatively private existence within the community. A comparison of the attitudes of More and Starkey in England with those of their contemporaries Erasmus and Pico della Mirandola in Europe reveals the extent to which England at first resisted the movement towards inwardness and solitude. For Pico, the inner world of the individual considered in isolation embodied the divine spark in man. Cultivation of 'things reasonable & civil' may make him celestial, but 'if he exalt the beautiful gift of his mind, to things

invisible and divine, hee transfourmeth himselfe into an Angel; and
to conclude, becommeth the sonne of God'.[30] For Starkey, by
contrast, the outward, social movement is more godlike than the
inward movement. According to him, man most resembles God in
applying his talents to the common good, since God's goodness 'is by
this chiefly declared and opened to the world, that to every thing
and creature He giveth part thereof according to their nature and
capacity'.[31]

The lives and works of these four men, More, Starkey, Erasmus
and Pico, all have some bearing on the debate concerning the
scholar's duty to put his knowledge to public use. Starkey's *Dialogue*
portrays Thomas Lupset trying to persuade Reginald Pole to
participate in affairs of government. Erasmus, despite holding
nominal public offices, was notoriously aloof, and may well have
been the model for Raphael in More's *Utopia*, the scholar who is
unwilling to sacrifice his retirement in order to counsel any prince.
A letter of Pico's, translated by More, sets out Pico's reasons for
refusing to become a counsellor, and it seems equally possible that
More could have used Pico's letter in shaping his Raphael, since
both argue for personal preference and individual liberty above the
duty to the common weal. Pico confesses to valuing 'my little house,
my study, the pleasure of my bokes, the rest and peace of my
mynde'[32] more highly than any moral arguments. The difference
between More and Pico is that More, although he shares Pico's
personal taste for privacy, values his sense of duty more highly.
Critics have argued over whether More speaks through the
character More or the character Raphael; but the answer is surely
that he is both of them, not just in the sense that he is author of both,
but in the sense that they enact the psychomachia between social
duty and personal preference in his own mind. The character More
is in no doubt about which of these alternatives is morally superior,
and tells Raphael: ' . . . it seems to me you will do what is worthy of
you and of this generous and truly philosophic spirit of yours if you
so order your life as to apply your talent and industry to the public
interest, even if it involves some personal disadvantages to yourself.'[33] The writer More finally made up his mind to such a course
two years after the publication of *Utopia*, when he gave up his
intellectual unattachment to take his place in the king's council.[34]

The debate on counsel, then, the sixteenth-century version of the
medieval debate on the active and contemplative lives, preoccupied
writers all over Europe; but the emphasis and conclusions most

commonly expressed in England were less individualistic than elsewhere. So pronounced was the English idealism of the common weal that some critics have considered that it reduced the individual to a mere vehicle for the attainment of the perfect state.[35] But this is to distort explicit statements of the time, which exalt the perfect state only in so far as it provides the conditions for the virtuous life of the individual. In Starkey's words, 'the end of all politic rule is to induce the multitude to virtuous living, according to the dignity of the nature of man.'[36] The perfect state was not idealised at the expense of the perfect individual, nor *vice versa*; writers retained the medieval ideal of a perfect balance between the two, the mutual fulfilment of each through the other.

What differentiates the early sixteenth-century writers from their medieval forebears and leaves them vulnerable to such distortion is their faith in the commonwealth as the *only* possible means to individual fulfilment and virtuous life. The bond between the individual and the state has here become absolute, in theory if not in practice, and exceptions are no longer tolerated, even for religious reasons. Sir Thomas Elyot's affirmation of the absolute necessity for participation in the universal order outside and beyond the self embodies the conviction of an age: ' . . . in thynges subjecte to Nature nothynge of hym selfe onely may be norisshed; but whan he hath distroyed that where with he dothe participate by the ordre of his creation, he hym selfe of necessite muste than perisshe, whereof ensuethe universall dissolution.'[37]

2 The Cult of Solitude

It was not until the late sixteenth century in England that personal preference and the particular nature of the individual began to take precedence over duty and obedience to the collective principle of nature, the common denominator of the characteristics most widely shared among men. This movement can be seen as early as the fourteenth century in Italy, however, in the person of Petrarch (1304–74).[1] In both his life and his work Petrarch was a great innovator. He was the first to write a book, *De Vita Solitaria*, on the subject of the pleasures of secular solitude. Although the incidental praise of solitary places or dispraise of the court can be found before Petrarch, no one before Petrarch had thought fit to devote an entire treatise to the joys of solitude *per se* without other motivation than the delights it had to offer. Petrarch also initiated the idea that the individual self was a worthy topic to write on, again simply for its own sake rather than for exceptional heroism or outstanding circumstances. Introspection reached an unprecedented level in his *Secretum*, which firmly established the link between the inward, self-analytical character and the desire for solitude, a link that was to be made repeatedly by later writers.

His ascent of Mount Ventoux gives some indication of the striking originality of his life and thought. Climbing a mountain simply for the view and for the inherent value of the experience seems to have been exceptional. A shepherd whom he meets on the way confirms this when he tells Petrarch that he knows of no one beside himself who has climbed the mountain: 'se . . . nec unquam aut ante illud tempus aut postea auditum apud eos quenquam ausum esse similia'[2] ('Never . . . had he heard that anyone else either before or after had ventured to do the same'[3]).

Although Petrarch did not climb the mountain alone, he clearly chose his brother as the companion who would least intrude on the private, inner experience. On reaching the top, he tells us, he opened his copy of Augustine's *Confessions* at random and felt rebuked by what he read there:

> 'Et eunt homines admirari alta montium et ingentes fluctus maris et latissimos lapsus fluminum et occeani ambitum et giros siderum, et relinquunt se ipsos'.

> ('Men go to admire the high mountains and the great flood of the seas and the wide-rolling rivers and the ring of Ocean and the movements of the stars; and they abandon themselves!')

From then on his inner solitude is total:

> Tunc vero montem satis vidisse contentus, in me ipsum interiores oculos reflexi, et ex illa hora non fuit qui me loquentem audiret donec ad ima pervenimus.

> (Then, sated with the sight of the mountain, I turned my inward eyes upon myself, and from that time no one heard me utter a word until we got to the bottom.)

When they return to the inn Petrarch does not even then become sociable and civil, but retires to a private room to write the letter in which he gives this account of his experience.

Petrarch's pursuit of privacy was no passing whim, but a deeply-rooted, almost obsessive facet of his character throughout most of his life. His contemporaries, to whom he was a celebrated public figure, possessed of all the opportunities afforded by fame and wealth in the city, could not understand his retirement to the relative hardship of a secluded country life at Vaucluse. Literary retirement became a cliché after Petrarch, but it was considered very eccentric in Petrarch's own day. It corresponded too with a changing relationship between writers, their works and their audience. Petrarch marked a turning point between the writer who wrote primarily for his audience, aiming to please and teach them (a theory still propounded by Sidney in his *Defence of Poesie* at the end of the sixteenth century in England) and the writer who writes primarily for himself, aiming to describe the truth about himself and to come to know himself better (a notion not really established in England until the seventeenth century). Petrarch makes this changing priority explicit in one of his letters:

Ceterum quid michi in his quantislibet vite mortalis angustiis sepius repetendum veniat, quam quod nunquam ex animo nisi cum anima discedet? Is est autem otii ac solitudinis appetitus, de quibus hactenus singulos tractatus edidi non tam aliis quam michi, ne forte silentium oblivio consecuta novis animum implicaret affectibus, a quo metu iam procul esse videor; sic mea mecum crevit opinio iamque induruit atque percalluit et in habitum versa est.[4]

(In these distresses of mortal existence I must constantly repeat my obsessing theme: the quest for peace and solitude. I have already written two treatises on the subject, not so much for others' profit as for my own, for fear that new cares might induce forgetfulness. That does not seem likely to happen. My conviction has increased with time: it has become so hard and tough that it is a rooted habit.[5])

Petrarch was well aware of the novelty of his own views and of the minority of men to whom they would appeal. It is easy to see how just this acknowledgement of exclusiveness could foster a cult. The superior tone of Petrarch's elitism in *De Vita Solitaria* indeed shows him almost consciously instigating such a cult: '. . . paucos quibus loquor, affuturos scio preter numerum superiores rebus omnibus atque victores'[6] ('I know that the chosen few to whom I address myself will be on my side and they are in all respects but numbers superior and triumphant over the rest'[7]).

There is, however, a certain conflict in his desires, which occasionally prompts him to write of his compulsion to return to the city or his ability to endure life at Vaucluse only temporarily (though it is important to note the distance at which Petrarch still stands from writers like Sir Thomas More or Seneca: his conflict is not between duty and desire, but between opposing desires). This alternation of attitudes has been taken as justification for presenting Petrarch as balancing between the civil and solitary lives, and committed to neither;[8] but this is to ignore Petrarch's own consistent description of himself as preoccupied with solitude. Writing to the Bishop of Cavaillon to introduce his *De Vita Solitaria*, he asks rhetorically:

Quid vero nunc prius ex me speres, quam quod et in ore et in corde semper habui, et ipse qui modo sub oculis est locus hortatur? solitarie scilicet otioseque vite preconium.[9]

(What now do you expect of me other than what I have always had in my mouth and in my heart, and what is preached by the very place I am now looking on—the celebration of a life of solitude and leisure.[10])

Although he appears to have planned a treatise on the active life to balance the *De Vita Solitaria*, it is surely significant that he never wrote it, producing instead two treatises on the solitary life, religious and secular. Everywhere in his letters he alludes to his love of solitude as a topic familiar to his friends; and in his *Secretum* he portrays Augustine rebuking him for false pride in deviating from the common path by his cultivation of solitude.

In the *Secretum*, of course, since it is in dialogue form, Petrarch the writer speaks *against* the solitary life through Augustine as well as representing his own solitary life through the character Petrarch. The introspective individual necessarily exhibits a form of self-division, since he must play both the observer and the observed. The self-division, though, is associated with his inwardness, his solitary tendency to take himself for company. Petrarch self-consciously bemoans this state of inner division, particularly in his sonnets, where he blames love for dividing him from himself. Many of the sonnets take the form of dialogues between different aspects of the self, and the language is full of reflexive actions, compulsively translated in English by compound words with 'self'. The imagery of Narcissus and the mirror also implies a self split in two, and this language and imagery of solipsism and division, together with the lover's need for physical solitude, dominate both Petrarch's sonnet sequence and those of his Elizabethan imitators. It is partly due to Petrarch's influence that the ideas of solitude, solipsism and self-division are so closely associated in Renaissance English literature, and specifically, of course, in Shakespeare.

Three aspects in particular of Petrarch's attitude to solitude separated him from the medieval perspective: his search for motivation primarily in his own character rather than in external causes; his valuing of personal preference and individual nature above collective morality and the general nature of mankind; and the purely secular nature of the solitude he sought. These changes together herald a movement away from the external world towards a higher esteem for the internal, individual world.

Medieval writers usually considered the state of solitude to be motivated by some accident of fortune or some particular state of mind, such as love, grief, madness, or religious fervour. Burton, as late as 1621 in England, continued to examine these external motivations at the same time as recognising the purely internal and spontaneous 'motivation', in his *Anatomy of Melancholy*. Petrarch was the first to confess to a desire for solitude simply for its own sake. Although occasionally he looks for external causes, such as love or civil unrest, he most often writes of it as an inner compulsion, or as he phrases it in one letter, 'latens animo calcar'[11] ('some inward spur'[12]).

Judging by his letters, his baffled friends often asked him to try to rationalise this 'inward spur', but the motivations Petrarch finds in answer are nearly always those of personal character and taste. He explains one preference by means of another preference:

> vel amore literarum amicum otio et literis locum amo, vel fortasse odio quodam ex dissimilitudine morum orto populum fugio, et fortasse conscientia vite mee multiloquum testem vito.[13]

> (My love of a spot favourable to literary leisure springs no doubt from my love of books, or perhaps I seek to escape from the crowd because of an aversion arising from a discrepancy in our tastes, or it may even be that from a squeamishness of conscience I like to avoid a many-tongued witness of my life.[14])

Petrarch revolutionised the terminology of the solitude debate, replacing the terminology of right and wrong, morally superior and inferior, more and less pleasing to God (terms familiar from medieval debate over the active and contemplative lives), with a new terminology of personal will, individual nature, and more and less pleasing to self. He leaves the reader in no doubt in his *De Vita Solitaria* that his aim in choosing the solitary life is personal happiness, not moral perfection. Like Seneca, he justifies his choice not by the law of universal nature, but by the freedom of his individual nature:

> nos de nobis libret unusquisque quid preferat; impossibile est enim, etsi unum omnes finem ultimum intendamus, et unam omnibus vite viam expediat sequi. Qua in re cuique acriter

cogitandum erit qualem eum natura, qualem ipse se fecerit.[15]

(let each man decide according to his own preference, for it is impossible that it should suit all men to follow a single road in life, even if they were all bound for the same ultimate destination. In this connection each man must seriously take into account the disposition with which nature has endowed him and the bent which by habit or training he has developed.[16])

The valuing of personal preference and particular character above a notional absolute of what is right for all men leads naturally to a secularism which locates truth within the inner man rather than in a God outside him. Hitherto, solitude had been associated with the search for God through contemplation; by examining his own soul, a man could come to know God. But Petrarch now secularised that contemplative solitude and offered self-examination not as a means to a higher end, but as an alternative, as an end in itself. He formulates the challenge in the first words of *De Vita Solitaria*:

Credo ego generosum animum, preter Deum ubi finis est noster, preter seipsum et archanas curas suas, aut preter aliquem multa similitudine sibi coniunctum animum, nusquam acquiescere.[17]

(I believe that a noble spirit will never find repose save in God, in whom is our end, or in himself and his private thoughts, or in some intellect united by a close sympathy with his own.[18])

God is offered as one of three possible ways towards self-fulfilment, and clearly, despite the occasional gesture in the direction of religion, it was not the alternative Petrarch chose. The very existence of the treatise *De Otio Religioso*, avowedly on religious solitude, suggests that *De Vita Solitaria* dealt with another kind of solitude. This is not, of course, to suggest that Petrarch was an irreligious man, but simply that religion was not the motivating force behind his search for solitude. He valued solitude for its ˙pleasures and its opportunities for self-examination and cultivation of the inner life, and these were for him self-justifying ends, not means towards other ends.

THE CHANGING FASHION IN ENGLAND

Early sixteenth-century English writers were united in the belief that the state was the only vehicle through which the individual might achieve fulfilment. Petrarch, on the other hand, believed withdrawal from an active civil life to be the only way to achieve any of the three types of fulfilment outlined at the beginning of *De Vita Solitaria* (p. 19 above). Late sixteenth-century England can be viewed as a battleground for these opposing ideals. Literature in praise of solitude became fashionable in England from about 1570, first in the form of translations from European writers and gradually in the original work of English writers. By 1605 the praise of solitude was, according to Bacon, a well-established and popular theme:

> And as for the privateness or obscureness (as it may be in vulgar estimation accounted) of life of contemplative men; it is a theme so common to extol a private life, not taxed with sensuality and sloth, in comparison and to the disadvantage of a civil life, for safety, liberty, pleasure, and dignity, or at least freedom from indignity, as no man handleth it but handleth it well; such a consonancy it hath to men's conceits in the expressing and to men's consents in the allowing.[19]

But solitude was more than just a popular literary theme. The existence of a cult of solitude can be inferred from the way in which it is so frequently linked with other recognised cults of the period. Indeed, any affectation, any cultivation of 'singularity', was inherently likely to seek out physical solitude as an expression of difference or aloofness from the rest of society.[20] Elizabethans recognised solitude as in some sense a metaphor for any cult and simultaneously condemned solitude as being an affectation and affectation in general as being anti-social. 'Al kinde of strangnes and particular humors', writes James Cleland, echoing Montaigne, are 'enemies of conversation'.[21] Castiglione too, the acknowledged authority on social conduct, warns against affectation of any kind.[22] Solitude can be seen thus either as a cult in its own right or as a focus for all cults, which in any case the Elizabethans mixed together indiscriminately. Lodge's *Wits Miserie*, for example, attempts to classify 'the Devils Incarnat of this Age'. But in one single character, fairly arbitrarily labelled 'Scandal & Detraction', he compounds the vices of pugnaciousness,

Machiavellianism, atheism, discontent, love of new-fangledness, a preference for travel, hatred of the commonwealth, conspiracy and rebelliousness. With such an amalgam of anti-social affectations in his character, it is no surprise to learn that this type also cultivates solitude: ' . . . if he walke Poules [Paul's], he sculks in the backe Isles, and of all things loveth no societies'.[23]

The plays of the 1590s and early 1600s are full of affected solitaries. The affectedness of Armado in *Love's Labour's Lost* (1594–5, revised 1597) expresses itself in his attempt to separate himself from the masses, to be 'singuled from the barbarous' (v. i. 68–9) both literally and metaphorically. Romeo's movement from the mere affectation of love for Rosaline to a more natural love for Juliet is marked by a return to sociability, as Mercutio remarks: 'Now art thou sociable, now art thou Romeo' (*Rom.* (1595–6), II. iv. 86). The purging of Macilente's humour at the end of Ben Jonson's *Every Man Out of His Humour* (1599) is similarly marked by his increased sociability. The meeting between the affected lover (Orlando) and the affected malcontent (Jaques) in *As You Like It* (1599) produces a conversation that parodies the expectation that each of them should adopt a solitary pose:

> *Jaq.* I thank you for your company, but, good faith,
>   I had as lief have been myself alone.
> *Orl.* And so had I; but yet, for fashion sake, I thank
>   you too for your society.
> *Jaq.* God buy you, let's meet as little as we can.
> *Orl.* I do desire we may be better strangers.
>
> (*AYL*, III. ii. 238–43)

The word 'fashion' draws attention here to the fashion-consciousness of these two, who are trying to outdo fashion (in the sense of convention) with fashion (in the sense of the latest affectation). The parody is carried further by the fact that the two do not then part, but Jaques invites Orlando to carry out the traditionally solitary pursuit of railing in company with him: 'Will you sit down with me? and we two will rail against our mistress the world, and all our misery' (III. ii. 261–2).

A similar conversation in *The White Devil* (performed 1611) parodies the fashion for solitude and melancholy in the Jacobean period:

Lodovico. Shalt thou and I join housekeeping?
Flamineo.   Yes, content:
    Let's be unsociably sociable.
Lod. Sit some three days together, and discourse.
Fla. Only with making faces;
    Lie in our clothes.
Lod.   With faggots for our pillows.
Fla.   And be lousy.
Lod. In taffeta linings, that's genteel melancholy.[24]

Other literary forms outside drama make the topical reference to a contemporary cult of solitude even more overt. John Marston's satires, for example, show him adopting the pose of the malcontent, and standing aloof from society in order to rail on it. The solitary pose is immediately established in the dedication, which departs from the convention of paying homage to a noble patron in order to dedicate the work to his 'most esteemed and best beloved Selfe'.[25] Robert Greene describes in his *Repentance* (1592) for his own youth how he deliberately cultivated melancholy and its accompanying poses.[26] The anonymous author of *Leycesters Common-wealth* confirms that the affectation of solitude and discontent was a part of Elizabethan life, not just a literary invention, and dates the fashion from the second decade of Elizabeth's reign, that is, from the 1570s. The diatribe issues supposedly from a lady of the court, who says:

> I doe well remember . . . the first douzen yeares of her highnesse raigne, how happy, pleasant, and quiet they were, with all manner of comfort and consolation . . . now, there are so many suspitions, every where, for this thing and for that: as wee cannot tell whom to trust. So many melancholique in the Court, that seeme malecontented: so many complaining or suing for their friends that are in trouble: other slip over the Sea, or retire themselves upon the sudden . . . wee can never almost be merry one whole day together.[27]

The tone of this passage also conveys the familiar belief that the trend towards retirement was part of a widespread social degeneration (cf. pp. 23–4 and 28–9 below).

More incontrovertibly than the evidence of literature, perhaps, changes in architecture confirm a movement towards increased

privacy in the late sixteenth and seventeenth centuries. Mark
Girouard, though he argues that 'the idea that there was no privacy
in a mediaeval house is based on a total misreading of the mediaeval
plan',[28] does not contradict the view that Elizabethan and
Jacobean houses offered far greater opportunities for privacy, and
demonstrates this in his discussion of the changing functions of
withdrawing chambers and the increasing use of parlours instead of
great chambers. The coining of the word 'apartment', first recorded
as used by Evelyn in 1641, suggests the same tendency to think of a
room as a place cut off from the surrounding space and people, a
place in which to be, relatively, 'apart'. The growing preference for
solitude can be seen outside the house too, in the development of
lodges 'often built in secluded or remote situations, and . . . as a
result, lonely and romantic places—or for those unattracted by
loneliness, melancholy places'.[29] Girouard cites Sidney and
Shakespeare respectively on the attractive or melancholy solitude of
lodges.

Evelyn's diary records more than his own personal inclination for
solitude;[30] it also provides evidence of the way in which the
changing design of both houses and gardens catered increasingly for
the desire to be alone. Evelyn records, for example, that he has
'built . . . a study, made a fishpond, Iland and some other solitudes
& retirements at Wotton'[31] and he frequently admires the 'solitudes' in the grounds of other houses he visits. He approves too of
provision for solitude indoors, and remarks admiringly on the
extension of these facilities even to strangers and servants at Euston
in Suffolk.[32]

This growing fashion for solitude is indicative not simply of
changing preferences but of a changing morality, which valued the
private good above the public good. The changes in architectural
design simply confirm a changing set of priorities which had been
manifested in a less tangible way from about the middle of the
sixteenth century. Preachers and government alike denounced the
flocking of the rural gentry to London in the sixteenth century as a
sign of declining commitment to the common good and urged them
to return to their country houses and revive the hospitality which
had made the manor house a focus for the sense of community.
George Gascoigne was one of many who lamented this substitution
of private pleasure for public duty as the source of the disintegration
of contemporary society:

> The stately lord, which woonted was to kepe
> A court at home, is now come up to courte,
> And leaves the country for a common prey,
> To pilling, polling, brybing, and deceit:
> (Al which his presence might have pacified,
> Or else have made offenders smel the smoke.)[33]

This movement from country to city in the sixteenth century was only the first stage in the weakening of the social bond; the second stage, ironically, was manifested in a return to country houses in the seventeenth century, now as a means of retiring from social obligations and responsibilities in the city in order to find personal freedom and leisure.

By the seventeenth century, however, such retirement had gained moral respectability as well as desirability, and was no longer condemned as selfish, but admired in terms similar to the medieval praise of the contemplative life. Whereas in the sixteenth century retirement was seen as symptomatic of self-love, 'the most inhibited sin in the canon' (*AWW*, i. i. 136–7), and was at the centre of a cult which openly challenged conventional morality with the amoral principle of personal pleasure, it regained in the seventeenth century the sanction of religion and ceased to be unconventional. Moral superiority, not amoral individualism, is the keynote of the solitude praised in the lyrics of Marvell, Milton, Benlowes, Fairfax, Mildmay Fane, Katherine Philips and innumerable other poets of the mid-seventeenth century.

Inevitably, as solitude became morally respectable, it ceased to be the focus of a cult and became part of the establishment. The cult, in the strict sense of the word, lasted for only a relatively short time around the turn of the century. Webster, who joked about the fashion for unsociableness in *The White Devil* (see p. 22 above), described Bosola in *The Duchess of Malfi* (performed 1612–14) as affecting an 'out-of-fashion melancholy'.[34] Everard Guilpin, writing before the end of the sixteenth century, in 1598, suggested that the affectation of solitude was somewhat passé even then:

> But see yonder,
> One like the unfrequented Theater
> Walkes in darke silence, and vast solitude,
> Suited to those blacke fancies which intrude,
> Upon possession of his troubled breast:

But for blacks sake he would looke like a jeast,
For hee's cleane out of fashion.[35]

The transition in the status of solitude from daring amorality to
conventional moral respectability, and the change in emphasis from
physical affectation to inward contemplation can be clearly shown
through a comparison of three 'Characters' of the solitary printed
between 1614 and 1631. The first, Sir Thomas Overbury's
Character of 'A Melancholy Man' (1614),[36] is extremely traditio-
nalist in its condemnation of the solitary as a deviant from the
natural social order. It begins with the fact of solitariness: the
melancholy man is 'a strayer from the drove: one that nature made
sociable, because she made him man, and a crazed disposition hath
altered.' His contemplative bent is ridiculed as foolish and inadequate: ' . . . stragling thoughts are his content, they make him
dreame waking . . . He thinks busines, but never does any: he is all
contemplation no action.' Overbury follows Aristotle in judging
him to be finally inhuman and unnatural: ' . . . a man onely in
shew, but comes short of the better part; a whole reasonable soule,
which is mans chiefe preheminence, and sole mark from creatures
senceable.'

John Earle distinguishes in his Characters between the 'discon-
tented' and the 'contemplative' types of solitude, instead of lumping
them under the same general condemnation of 'Melancholy' as
Overbury does. Earle's 'Contemplative Man' (1628)[37] is justified,
almost deified, by his contemplations; his withdrawal is symptomatic of intellectual superiority rather than feebleness. This solitary
is 'a scholar in this great university the world; and the same his book
and study. He cloysters not his meditations in the narrow darkness
of a room.' His scorn of 'natural' man is justified by Earle as godlike
rather than bestial: 'He looks upon man from a high tower, and sees
him trulier at this distance in his infirmities and poorness. He scorns
to mix himself in men's actions, as he would to act upon a stage; but
sits aloft on the scaffold a censuring spectator.' His solitude is a
moral and religious state, leading towards heaven.

The moral transformation of the solitary is clear too in Wye
Saltonstall's Character of 'A Melancholy Man' (1631):[38] the label
no longer carries inherent condemnation, but rather inherent
admiration, based on the association of solitude with contemplative
superiority. This type is not totally solitary, but avoids extreme
sociability, and his solitary bent is seen as an expression of his

sincerity and his justifiable contempt for the opinion of the masses. His anti-social manner is the natural consequence of great intellect: 'If he walke and see you not, 'tis because his mind being busied in some serious contemplation, the common sense has no time to judge of any sensuall object.' The eccentricity of the solitary, a source of ridicule and sign of affectation for Overbury, has now come to be taken as evidence of a praiseworthy preoccupation with spiritual matters. The fashionable, uncompromising and defiant pose of the Elizabethan age has been modified to become the established moral and religious ideal of the Caroline period.

THE SOLITUDE WITHIN

The idea of physical solitude has always implied metaphysical solitude, and it is this spiritual state of detachment or self-enclosure which has aroused the widest range of moral responses. The passion with which men argued either for or against physical solitude in the sixteenth and seventeenth centuries can only be understood by recognising that physical solitude was a metaphorical focus for an attitude both to the self and to society. Donne, for example, arguing about physical solitude in *Biathanatos*, uses the topic as a vehicle for a more abstract consideration of moral values. His justification of physical solitude is really a plea for the freedom and autonomy of the individual as against the moral laws established for society as a whole. Marshalling both scriptural and classical authorities, Donne argues thus:

> For we know that (a) 'some things are naturall to the *species*, and other things to the particular *person*' and that the latter may correct the first. And therefore when (b) *Cicero* consulted the oracle at *Delphos*, he had this answer, 'Follow your owne nature'. And so certainly that place, (c) 'It is not good for the man to be alone' is meant there, because if he were alone, Gods purpose of multiplying mankinde had beene frustrate. Yet though this be ill for conservation of our *species* in generall, yet it may be very fit for some particular man, to abstaine from all such conversation of marriage or men, and retire to a sollitude.[39]

Though sociability may be recommended for mankind in general, Donne argues, individual exceptions to the rule may be justified.

Thus the argument in defence of physical solitude for certain individuals becomes an argument in defence of a general principle whereby an individual stands morally alone and makes his choices on the basis of inner conviction, a sense of what is right for himself, not on the basis of those generally agreed principles which are evolved in accordance with the ideal of the common good. 'A private man', according to Donne's arguments, is not inflexibly bound by collective moral law, but 'Emperor of himselfe'.[40]

This standpoint is a complete reversal of the early sixteenth-century belief that the individual should be bound by collective morality and the principle of the common good in all his choices. A man could not at that period convince others that his notion of what was right for him alone was morally acceptable; right and wrong were not seen as relative, varying according to each individual, but absolute, determined by the notion of the common weal. This changing focus in moral thinking from the early to the late sixteenth century produced an increasing self-awareness in the individual and a growing sense of the world outside the self as relative, as a subjective experience rather than an objective absolute. The idea that physical factors are not fixed, that 'It is the mynd, that maketh good or ill',[41] became a cliché, and the image of man as a microcosm was turned on its head. Donne, as might be expected from his argument for individual autonomy in *Biathanatos*, is one of those who comments on the inadequacy of this traditional image. He writes:

> It is too little to call man a little world; except God, man is a diminutive to nothing. Man consists of more pieces, more parts, than the world; than the world doth, nay, than the world is. And if those pieces were extended, and stretched out in man as they are in the world, man would be the giant, and the world the dwarf; the world but the map, and man the world.[42]

As more attention was turned inwards, towards the immeasurable powers of the mind, so the traditional cosmic hierarchy had to be reassessed. Men could no longer accept a system which enclosed them, but rather emphasised how such systems could be punctured by the capacity of the individual mind to contain them.

Yet this power of the mind to subdue and enclose objective reality could be seen either as liberating man and making him godlike,[43] or as restricting and isolating him. Increased self-awareness was not necessarily an escape from subjection: it could equally well be viewed simply as the exchange of one prison for another. Instead of giving the individual a sense of freedom and exultation in having escaped from the prison of a rigid cosmic order, it might give him a sense of claustrophobia, a sense that in escaping from that framework to one determined by the self he had merely narrowed his prison, forcing the whole world to become a reflection of the self. Bacon, for one, was disgusted by the kinds of imprisonment and limitation a man might bring on himself by worship of his own subjectivity. The image, 'Idols of the Cave', which he uses to describe these false values, suggests their capacity to isolate the individual. Bacon explains the folly of these false idols in *The New Organon* (1620). Everyone, he says,

> . . . (besides the errors common to human nature in general) has a cave or den of his own, which refracts and discolours the light of nature; owing either to his own proper and peculiar nature; to his education and conversation with others; or to the reading of books, and the authority of those whom he esteems and admires; or to the differences of impressions, accordingly as they take place in a mind preoccupied and predisposed or in a mind indifferent and settled; or the like. So that the spirit of man (according as it is meted out to different individuals) is in fact a thing variable and full of perturbation, and governed as it were by chance. Whence it was well observed by Heraclitus that men look for sciences in their own lesser worlds, and not in the greater or common world.[44]

The vocabulary of Bacon's last sentence makes it quite clear that for him the microcosm image puts matters in their right perspective. It is arrogance mingled with stupidity on man's part, he implies, that leads him to elevate his own position in nature.

Physical solitude is not only the image of involuntary isolation, such as this isolation of self-awareness and subjectivity, but of the more voluntary forms of isolation, like self-love and detachment from the concerns of mankind as a whole. The figure of Narcissus was often taken as a type of wilful solitariness, and Bacon's explication of the myth of Narcissus in *Of the Wisdom of the Ancients* (1609) makes explicit the link between the spiritual isolation of self-love and actual physical withdrawal from society:

For with this state of mind there is commonly joined an indisposition to appear much in public or engage in business; because business would expose them to many neglects and scorns, by which their minds would be dejected and troubled. Therefore they commonly live a solitary, private, and shadowed life.[45]

Bacon's moral condemnation of such withdrawal, whether physical, spiritual, or both, also comes through strongly in the tone of this passage.

Moral condemnation of withdrawal from social obligations was naturally strong in sermons, which also condemned it as a form of self-love. The rejection of social bonds by a few individuals was seen as the source of all social decay and as heralding the end of the world. The prophetic tone of this sermon by Charles Pynner (printed in 1597) is characteristic of a tone of pessimism which was as widespread in the period as the enthusiasm and optimism which are perhaps more frequently taken as typical:

> . . . the father, oweth more to the childe; the husband, to the wife; the brother, to his brother; yea, the friende to his friende; (because hee hath bounde him by a speciall band) then to any other. And if these will not honor these, protect and defend, helpe, comfort, and nourish these, (as too often we may see this honor wanting) it is because we are fallen into the last times; of which the Apostle forewarned they should be greevous.[46]

The chain is clear and irrevocable for Pynner: the individual puts himself before his kindred and friends, thus denying his bond with his fellow men, relationships break down, society disintegrates and the decline leads eventually to the end of the world.

The solitary was not necessarily self-loving, of course; self-love was a loaded term adopted by the moralists in order to condemn solitude. The position of the solitary might more faithfully be categorised as self-defining, a quality more difficult to judge in moral terms. The solitary's rejection of social bonds was symptomatic of a wish to be defined from within rather than by external context, by his place in society or in creation as a whole. Two quotations from the Bible may be set against each other to suggest the ambiguity of Scripture as an authority concerning self-definition: God's own self-definition, 'I AM THAT I AM' (Exod. 3:14) and St Paul's qualification of this, 'by the grace of God, I am that I am' (1

Cor. 15:10). The qualification is what prevents St Paul's assertion from being read as a heretical challenge to God, but when the phrase is echoed by Renaissance characters it is not so easy to judge its tone. Richard III's 'I am' does not stand alone in its time, but must be measured against, for example, the motto of Sidney's Pamela in the *Arcadia* (1590): 'yet still my selfe',[47] or the self-appointed virtue of Marston the satirist: 'I am my selfe'.[48] The aspiration towards self-definition is a characteristic shared by a wide variety of characters and one that, like solitariness, evokes both admiration and condemnation.

Such solipsism echoes the position of the writer himself.[49] Writers in this period become much more concerned to express their inward selves and less concerned with didactic, outward-looking aims. Where the usual justification of a work of literature had been its capacity to improve men, the act of writing was now increasingly regarded as self-justifying, valid simply as self-expression. Montaigne draws attention to the relative novelty of this way of looking at literature in describing his own *Essays*:

> I have presented my selfe unto my selfe for a subject to write, and argument to descant upon. It is the only booke in the world of this kinde, and of a wilde extravagant designe. Moreover, there is nothing in it worthy the marking but this fantasticalnesse.[50]

As late as 1643, Sir Kenelm Digby seemed still perplexed by such a circular activity and wrote after reading Sir Thomas Browne's *Religio Medici*: 'What should I say of his making so particular a narration of personall things, and privat thoughts of his owne: the knowledge whereof can, not much conduce to any mans better-ment? which I make account is the chiefe end of his writing this discourse.'[51] Yet Digby understood the impulse better than he pretends, since he had already written an autobiography of his own, mostly written in 1628, which he described as 'begun only for my own recreation, and then continued and since preserved only for my own private content',[52] thus explicitly endorsing the solipsistic motive.

The upsurge of autobiography in this period is an illustration of the preoccupation with the self, and the continued exhibition of a preference for solitude on the part of autobiographers helps to confirm the link between solitude and the introspective tendency, already exhibited in Petrarch. Digby, while expressing his willingness to accept public employment if his services are required, confessed 'that retiredness would afford me much more solid content, especially in these depraved times';[53] Lord Herbert of Cherbury admitted: 'I ever loved my book, and a private life, more than any busy preferments';[54] Sir Thomas Bodley expressed gratitude for 'my retired course of Life, which is now methinks to me, as the greatest Preferment that the State can afford';[55] and the Duchess of Newcastle described herself as 'addicted from my childhood to contemplation rather than conversation, to solitariness rather than society'.[56]

The desire for solitude increasingly became associated with great intellect through its links with the pursuits of writing and study. Whereas in the medieval period Aristotle's designation of the solitary as either a god or a beast was read as a condemnation of all solitude except that of religious contemplatives, it was more often read in the seventeenth century as an invitation to the individual to become godlike by cultivating his mind in the isolation of the inner world. 'Cogitation', wrote Abraham Cowley, 'is the thing which distinguishes the Solitude of a God from a wild Beast';[57] and Thomas Nashe explained the cult of solitude as an attempt to appear intellectual:

Some think to be counted rare politicians and statesmen by being solitary; as who should say, 'I am a wise man, a brave man, *Secreta mea mihi; Frustra sapit, qui sibi non sapit* [My secrets are my own; he is wise in vain who does not know his own business], and there is no man worthy of my company or friendship'.[58]

Intellectual superiority now became an alternative to spiritual superiority in the seventeenth-century justification of solitude. While contemplation remained the natural occupation of the solitary, as it had been in the Middle Ages, the focus of that contemplation could be either God or the individual self. For the medieval hermit solitude was righteous only if it led to God, and godless solitude was an outrage against both man and God; but for the seventeenth-century solitary, as for Petrarch, God was only one possible object of his contemplation, and not necessarily the motivation behind his solitary state, even though it might retain a religious veneer. Religion, from having been a prerequisite for praiseworthy solitude, became merely an optional addition to it.

3 'Single nature's double name'

DIVISION

The usurpation of social ideals by a growing preference for solitude and an increasing emphasis on the inner life did not follow a clear, graduated movement. The earliest stages of transition, in the period that roughly coincided with Shakespeare's lifetime, were characterised by uncertainty, inconsistency and ambiguity. It is the purpose of this chapter to correct any impression that may have been formed from Chapter 2 that writers of this period could be simply divided into those for and those against solitude. On the contrary, the same individuals can be found praising solitude at one point, who condemn it at another. This apparent self-contradiction arose partly out of the conflict between personal preference and moral conviction, since the attractions of solitude were clearly felt long before it acquired moral respectability. What appears to be self-contradiction is thus more accurately described as a confusion between two separate arguments: whether the solitary life is more pleasurable than the civil life, and whether it is morally superior to it. It was on the whole not until the seventeenth century that writers distinguished explicitly between 'what is lawful in it self' and 'what is convenient for us'.[1] Lodowyck Bryskett, writing probably in the late 1580s, is exceptional among sixteenth-century writers in his clear-sighted recognition of this distinction. In his *Discourse on Civill Life* (not printed until 1606), which takes the form of a conversation between Bryskett and several friends, Bryskett portrays himself as admitting to a preference for a life of seclusion and study, but continuing:

> . . . yet do I not therin contradict the reasonable and just disposition I have to employ my selfe for the service of her Majestie, when occasion serveth: neither doth my endevour in

that behalf any way oppose it selfe to my desire, of retiring from a painefull employment to a more quiet life . . . And were it but in regard of that same contentment, I know not what man of reasonable sense and understanding, would not esteeme the purchase thereof at a farre higher rate then any office . . . whatsoever.[2]

Most writers did not separate moral arguments from arguments of pleasure in this way, but tried to answer moral objections with reference to the criteria of individual taste and character. Those defending solitude in the early period seemed to feel its moral dubiousness as strongly as those attacking it, and there was a tendency to excuse rather than justify solitude, an attempt to make it acceptable by making it resemble the social life in some strained way. Thus physical solitude might be defended on the grounds of some selfless motivation, such as loving men too much to endure the sight of their vices, or studying in private in order to benefit men by the knowledge so acquired. Paradoxes, such as Scipio's legendary saying, 'Numquam minus solus quam cum solus'[3] (Never less alone than when alone), or the opposite idea, of being most alone when in a crowd, were useful ways of blurring the opposition between solitude and society. Even the vocabulary in which arguments in favour of solitude were framed tended to blur the distinctions. Rather than use a terminology which made explicit the challenge to traditional morality inherent in the exaltation of solitude as an ideal, writers preferred to disguise the challenge by using the vocabulary of the old morality, words like 'nature', 'order', 'law', 'reason', and gradually twisting the words themselves in the course of their discussion. The words themselves thus lost all precision in expanding to accommodate senses which actually contradicted each other and allowed writers room to remain evasive and ambiguous.

The definition of 'solitude' itself became similarly fluid. Petrarch admits to a looseness in his usage of the Latin 'solitudo' in his *De Vita Solitaria*, defining the solitude in which he is interested as 'eam . . . solitudinem . . . non que unum etiam sed que turbas fugit'[4] (that solitude which flees not the individual but the crowds). Roger Baynes, in *The Praise of Solitarinesse*, shows the same sense of the word's fluidity, and portrays one of his speakers asking the other:

. . . whether you intend *Solitarinesse* to consist in that, that a man withdrawing himselfe from company, seeketh rather to live in the voide and desolate places of the earth, and there, playing the Philosopher in the open wildernesse, doth seeme alone to contente hymselfe: or that you deeme, the substance thereof to remayne in the common societie of man, notwithstanding, to be conversaunt but with few.[5]

Sir John Harington, with airy disregard for any notion of objective meaning, actually defines solitude as a middle way between extremes:

Therefore concludinge we saye that such a solytude as we commende, is neyther to mingle with the multytude, nor be so retyred as to deserve the name of inhumayne . . . For whoe so excludeth all companie, shall finde solitude extreamly sower and irksome. My solitude therefore shall not be troubled with the companie of frendes but rather comforted. Fynally, yf needes I must forgoe all companie, then had I rather forsake solytude, then be left all alone.[6]

Solitude (or 'solitariness(e)', the common Elizabethan form) is a relative term, varying according to context. It can suggest the country life, the contemplative life, the melancholy humour, the refusal of public office, the studious disposition. It can be classified, as it was by contemporaries, as referring to time, place or the mind. It can be voluntary or involuntary, and thereby associated with either freedom or imprisonment. It can be an expression of self-love, love of the community, or love of God. The flexibility of its semantic range is symptomatic of the uncertainty surrounding attitudes to it in this period.

Another symptom of this uncertainty was the popularity of the dialogue form, which enabled the writer to express both sides of every question without committing himself to either. It also enabled him to shift his ground subtly, allowing the same words to be interpreted differently by each speaker, and each speaker to modify his position to accommodate the objections of the other. Indeed, the characteristic movement of dialogues on solitude was from two simple and opposite positions, in which the terms 'solitude' and 'society' were interpreted fairly rigidly, through a series of qualifications, paradoxes, concessions and redefinitions, to a point of intersection where each of these opposites had been so modified that it could scarcely be distinguished from the other. Stefano Guazzo's *Civile Conversation* (translated 1581), for example, grants a Pyrrhic victory to the civil life, closing not with an emphatic statement of this conclusion, but with a list of exceptions to the general rule, types of solitude which are acceptable. Another anonymous treatise, *Cyvile and uncyvile Life* (1579), informs the reader in the preface that the conclusion in favour of the civil life is a more or less arbitrary choice, and that the 'uncivil' life is in reality equally faultless. 'It shall therfore please me', the writer continues, 'that every man please him selfe, usinge the liberty and will of his owne minde: and though it be farre diverse from mine, yet I know not why his opinion should trouble mee, or mine offende him'.[7]

Montaigne, who wavered between praising the pleasures of solitude and affirming his excessive sociability, confronted his own inconsistency: 'We float and waver betweene divers opinions: we will nothing freely, nothing absolutely, nothing constantly.'[8] He recognised his own compulsion towards the qualification of any statement, a compulsion shared, but not so openly acknowledged, by the English writers quoted above. 'I am drawn to hate likely things,' he wrote, 'when men goe about to set them downe as infallible. I love these words or phrases, which mollifie and moderate the temerity of our propositions: "It may be": "Peradventure": "In some sort": "Some": "It is said": "I thinke," and such like.'[9] Such acknowledgement of contradictory impulses and feelings of division can be found among English writers too. John Donne coined the two titles 'Jack Donne' and 'Dr Donne' to express his own sense of duality; Robert Burton opened his *Anatomy of Melancholy* with self-conscious contradiction:

'Tis my desire to be alone . . .
'Tis my sole plague to be alone

Naught so sweet as melancholy . . .
Naught so sad as melancholy.[10]

Sir Thomas Browne found comfort for his own sense of self-division in affirming such to be the necessary condition of man, 'that great and true *Amphibium*, whose nature is disposed to live not onely like other creatures in divers elements, but in divided and distinguished worlds'.[11] Bacon went further, believing duality to be a principle of all nature, and classifying the dichotomy as being between individual, self-contained existence, 'as every thing is a total or substantive in itself', and existence in context, 'as it is a part or member of a greater body'.[12] Such a principle implied that the conflict between solitary and social motivations was the essential basis of all nature; it is easy, then, to see why the debate on solitude was a vehicle for so many more abstract and all-embracing arguments about the nature of the individual and his place in society. Bacon in fact brings this empirical principle closer to the debate on solitude by using it to make a moral point in expressing the view that the second aspect of nature, the communal or collective, is 'the greater and the worthier, because it tendeth to the conservation of a more general form'.[13] Bacon's argument draws attention to another semantic paradox which was eroding the clear definition of a word: 'individual' was developing away from its root sense 'undividable' towards a suggestion of necessary division. 'Single nature's double name', as Shakespeare wrote in 'The Phoenix and the Turtle', 'Neither two nor one was called'.

The centrality of the division between the public and private, or communal and solitary, aspects of nature can be further illustrated in the way Renaissance writers tended to re-interpret older literature as portraying this division allegorically. The *Iliad*, the *Odyssey*, the *Aeneid* and *The Divine Comedy* were all read as allegories of either the active or the contemplative life or both. Tasso explains these interpretations in the Preface to his *Gerusalemme Liberata*, and announces a similar allegorical framework behind his own poem.[14] Spenser proclaims that he is following 'all the antique poets historical', Homer, Virgil, Ariosto and Tasso, in his plan to portray Arthur's 'private morall vertues' in his first twelve books and his 'polliticke vertues' in another twelve.[15] If all nature embodies a tension between the solitary and the social impulses, then all great literature must portray this same tension, either explicitly or allegorically: or such seems to have been the assumption behind such interpretations.

The opinion that division was inherent in all nature was only one rationalisation of the sense of self-division. Another possibility (disconcertingly embraced by some of the same writers who expressed the first opinion too) was that division was a condition of the times, and that the conflict within the individual was related to disorder in the macrocosm. The anti-social impulse towards solitude could then be viewed either as the source of social disorder (see p. 29 above) or as a response to it. Spenser continually laments the disorder of his times, and Donne's rueful "'Tis all in pieces, all coherence gone'[16] has been quoted so often as to have become one kind of epitaph for the times. Sermons harangue their audiences with the degeneracy of the contemporary world, and, though that can be partially dismissed as characteristic of sermons from any period, Elizabethan sermons are remarkably specific and topical about the evils they condemn.[17]

One new topic of complaint arising in the reign of Elizabeth which focused the fear that society was disintegrating was Machiavellianism. The machiavel, solitary, egotistic, dissembling, trusting himself alone, known fully to himself alone, was seen as both source and symptom of the weakening of the social bonds. Yet the division between his public and private selves which characterised the machiavel, his preference for his own individual good above the common good, his self-involved existence, were qualities presented without moral judgement, even admired, in other figures. Nowhere is the divided response to the solitary in the Elizabethan period seen more clearly than in the contrast between the judgements passed on Machiavelli's Prince, the model for the stage-villain, and Castiglione's Courtier, the model of ideal behaviour. Despite the apparent opposition between Machiavelli and Castiglione, their apparent approval of the solitary and the social type respectively, both writers actually recommend a similar spiritual solitariness. Both depict essentially isolated individuals in different moral disguises, and it is their Elizabethan readers who pretend to drive a moral wedge between them.

COURTIER AND PRINCE

Castiglione's *The Courtier* and Machiavelli's *The Prince* have been singled out by later ages as two of the most influential and representative books of the Renaissance. Both were Italian, both were written in the early sixteenth century, both had an immeasurable effect on later English literature. Both the Courtier and the Prince became cult figures in England, where they came to represent the extremes of moral perfection and corruption respectively. The ideal courtier of English courtesy books and the machiavellian villain of English drama seem at first sight totally opposed to each other: the one sociable, loyal, considerate, the other solitary, treacherous, egotistical. Where one strives towards an ideal of virtue, the other calculates how to cultivate the appearance of virtue to cloak his vice and exploits his cynical knowledge of how far other men fall short of their ideals. Where one seems to embody the social virtues, the other undermines the social fabric by presenting a false mask to society and retaining his self-love and inward disengagement from social concerns.

The originals of these caricatures are less distant from each other than the Elizabethans seemed to think. There is a fundamental difference between the aims of Castiglione and Machiavelli which is obscured by the highly moralistic English attitudes to both. Whereas Castiglione is explicitly formulating an ideal, Machiavelli is describing 'what men do and not what they ought to do'.[18] Machiavelli starts from the premiss that no men live up to their ideals, and suggests practical alternatives to idealism. Given that men are less than ideal in moral terms, the Prince must accommodate himself to this fact of life merely to survive:

> . . . soe greate is the difference betwene the lyves wee doe leade, and the lives wee shoulde leade: that he which respectes not what is doon, but studies onlie to learne that which shoulde be doon, is liker by his knowledge to purchase his owne subvertion, then by his conninge to provide for his safetie; for he that in everie respect will needes be a good man cannot choose but be overthrowne emonge soe many that are ill. It is necessarie therefore for a prince, yf he have regarde to his owne securitie, to knowe howe to be good and badd, and use both as the occasion of his accidentes, and necessitie of his causes shall require.[19]

Machiavelli distinguishes quite clearly here between the moral ideal and the political expedient: it is possible that, if his intention had been to describe the moral ideal, he might have depicted a man like Castiglione's Courtier. And it is possible that Castiglione might have admitted that more men were actually like those Machiavelli portrayed than like those he himself did.

In any case, Castiglione's ideal and Machiavelli's reality are not so different as they at first seem, though their closeness is masked by Castiglione's relative evasiveness. The Courtier and the Prince are not simply a social man and a solitary; they share an inward solitariness which reveals itself in their attitudes both to themselves and to society. Although the Prince is the only one to show a tendency to physical aloofness, such a state is to some extent forced on him by his position, as it is on Shakespeare's kings. Even Castiglione, while not encouraging physical solitariness in his Courtier, recognises the Prince's need for and right to privacy. The Courtier is instructed to respect the Prince's periods of solitude, and not to 'covet to presse into the chamber or other secrete places where his Lord is withdrawen'.[20]

The internal isolation of Machiavelli's Prince scarcely needs exemplifying, since it is so explicit. Like Petrarch and the solitaries of the Elizabethan cult, he communicates only with himself, not with other men. Machiavelli openly states that the primary motivation for all the Prince's actions is self-interest. The Courtier shares this self-dedication, and other manifestations of a spiritual isolation, but Castiglione blurs the issue by presenting the Courtier wholly in a social context. He describes the Courtier from the outside, as others see him, rather than from within, as Machiavelli describes the Prince, and implies by advising him to cultivate social qualities (duty, service, tact, decorum) that there is no conflict between his private and his public self, and that he is an individual devoted to the common weal. Yet this is not the case, for Castiglione's primary emphasis falls more on the cultivation than on the qualities to be cultivated, more on perfecting a social persona than on a feeling for the social order. The Courtier's motivation is self-loving rather than selfless: he seeks to please others in order to please himself finally, cultivates perfection for his own self-satisfaction and for the advancement that follows on such a reputation. Jacob Burckhardt's famous evaluation of Castiglione's Courtier emphasises his narcissistic qualities:

> He was the ideal man of society, and was regarded by the civilization of that age as its choicest flower; and the court existed for him far rather than he for the Court. Indeed, such a man would have been out of place at any Court, since he himself possessed all the gifts and bearing of an accomplished ruler, and because his calm supremacy in all things, both outward and spiritual, implied a too independent nature. The inner impulse which inspired him was directed, though our author does not acknowledge the fact, not to the service of the prince, but to his own perfection.[21]

Ironically, this interpretation of Castiglione would place self-love even higher on his scale of things than on Machiavelli's, for

Machiavelli's advocation of ruthless tyranny and dedication to political expediency before moral impeccability is the outcome of a patriotic belief that such forcefulness is the way to restore order and unity to Italy. Thus, while the Courtier seems more socially acceptable, his motives are essentially self-interested, and while the Prince seems to embody an egotism which is social anathema, Machiavelli's motive in depicting him thus is at least partly social.

The most striking difference between Castiglione and Machiavelli is in their degree of explicitness. Paradoxically, Machiavelli, who depicts a dissembler, is himself completely open about the the kind of man the Prince is, whereas Castiglione, who depicts a man who seems to be the ornament of any society, leaves the inner self of the Courtier to be inferred from his actions. Machiavelli describes amorality for what it is, and openly recommends a division between the private and public selves; Castiglione implies by what he does not say that the Courtier's private self is one with his public self, and blandly ignores the moral question of motivation. The morality of *The Courtier* is characterised by its omissions. Castiglione nowhere says that the Courtier should value the common good before his private good, nor that his aim should be to contribute to the social order. He appears not to care about the Courtier's feelings, only about his actual performance. His true distance from the medieval social ideal can be seen by contrast with Caxton's portrait of the ideal knight:

> To a knyght apperteyneth/ that he be a lover of the comyn wele/ For by the comynalte of the people was the chyvalrye founden and establyssed/ And the comyn wele is gretter and more necessary than propre good and specyall/[22]

or even by contrast with early sixteenth-century English writers like Elyot, Starkey and More.

The Courtier's social performance is no more the spontaneous expression of love for the common weal than the Prince's. Both are self-assertive showmen, more interested in the impression they make on their audience than in any co-ordination between that impression and their inner states. If truth, openness and sincerity are the basis of communication, relationships, and hence society, the Courtier is as anti-social as the Prince. He is required to speak the truth to his Prince, but Machiavelli's Prince demands as much from his courtiers. More frequently, the Courtier must dissemble, like the

Prince, and adapt himself according to the considerations of decorum, the time, place and persons. No matter what his mood, he must 'keepe companye pleasauntlye with every man' (p. 55) and 'consider wel what the thing is he doth or speaketh, the place wher it is done, in presence of whom, in what time, the cause why he doeth it' (p. 112). If he feels melancholy, he must dissemble for the sake of his Prince, and to preserve his own standing in the Prince's estimation, for he is never to be 'sad befor his prince, nor melancholy' (p. 124). He is no more spontaneous or natural than Machiavelli's Prince; in fact, Castiglione goes even further than Machiavelli in insisting that the Courtier should cultivate the appearance of spontaneity by adopting 'a certain Reckelesness, to cover art withall, and seeme whatsoever he doth and sayeth to do it wythout pain, and (as it were) not myndyng it' (p. 59). The difference again is only that whereas Machiavelli openly recognises that dissembling is politically necessary rather than morally acceptable, Castiglione appears not to notice any doubtfulness about the morality of the dissembling he recommends.

The measure both Courtier and Prince take of time, place and persons, though one calls it decorum and the other necessity, is also the measure of their detachment from society. However much they may appear to participate in an active civil life, the fact that their participation is a performance rather than a spontaneous expression of themselves demonstrates their self-enclosure, their reserving of the 'true' self for moments of solitary self-communion while cheating society with a mere mask. They feel no commitment to other men, but view them as an audience, a commodity, a set of objects to be manipulated for individual ends. Machiavelli openly voices his contempt for the social bonds, the bonds of love and loyalty rather than fear, 'for love', he writes, 'is conteyned under dutie, which for verie lighte occasion wicked men will violate, abusinge all meanes of pietie for anie kynde of proffitte' (pp. 72–3). Castiglione's opinion that the Courtier should 'keepe companye pleasauntlye with every man' (p. 55) has a hollow, superficial ring, and even his feeling that the Courtier should 'finde him oute an especiall and hartie friende, if it were possible, of that sort we have spoken of' (p. 138) sounds uncomfortably cold and practical, rather as though he were telling the Courtier to go out and buy any other commodity which would improve his image.

The Elizabethans, like Castiglione, either did not see or chose to ignore the moral ambivalence of the Courtier's behaviour, and displayed characteristic self-contradiction in admiring in him the same qualities that they condemned in Machiavelli's Prince. The inner solitude of the Courtier was made to seem acceptable by being presented in a context of external sociability, while the Prince's was rendered unacceptable by being presented openly and without compromise, explicitly linked with physical aloofness and contempt for the forms of sociability. The history of both these books in England shows clearly the gap in time between the acceptance of each. Both were translated in Elizabeth's reign, but translations of Machiavelli remained in manuscript, and probably circulated secretly, whereas Hoby's translation of Castiglione was published in 1561 and widely recommended as a book of moral excellence, even by one of such high standing, for example, as Roger Ascham,[23] once tutor to the young Elizabeth. No translation of Machiavelli was printed until 1640 (although Gentillet's tract against Machiavelli was printed in translation as early as 1602), by which time Machiavelli's view of natural man as solitary and self-interested, and society as an arbitrary and artificial restraint on man, was widespread. Whether the association of solitude with self-interest was deplored, as by Hobbes and the Calvinists, or its association with contemplation and innocence was admired, as by Henry Vaughan, Charles Cotton and the other retirement poets, the general attitude differed from that of the Elizabethans in that solitude was no longer seen by either group as unconventional or unnatural. The distance in time between the acceptance of *The Courtier* and *The Prince* reveals, like the rise and decline of the cult of solitude, a shift in the idea of natural man. Whereas in the Elizabethan period solitude was seen as daring, unconventional, often unnatural, and had to be disguised either as a caricature of itself or to resemble sociability, it had come to be accepted by the mid-seventeenth century as natural, and writers differed only in so far as they admired or condemned that natural inclination.

THE DRAMATIC SOLITARY

The Elizabethan response to Machiavelli is probably most familiar through the creation of the machiavellian villain in drama. Something of the ambiguity of the response is focused in this figure, who, although always a villain, always the object of moral condemnation, also elicits a kind of admiration which is totally divorced from moral judgement. Just as the same qualities are condemned in Machiavelli's Prince as are admired in Castiglione's Courtier, so the machiavellian villains of Elizabethan drama are condemned for characteristics shared by its heroes. The words 'hero' and 'villain' become highly ambiguous when used to refer to the drama of this period, since admiration so often works against moral judgement, so that a character can become a hero in some sense while being simultaneously acknowledged to be morally degenerate. Something of this mingling of admiration with moral condemnation is contained in this seventeenth-century commentary on *The White Devil*, addressed to Webster:

> *Brachianos* Ill,
> Murthering his Dutchesse, hath by thy rare skill
> Made him renown'd, *Flamineo* such another,
> The Devils darling, Murtherer of his brother:
> His part most strange, (given him to Act by thee)
> Doth gaine him Credit, and not Calumnie:
> *Vittoria Corombona*, that fam'd Whore,
> Desp'rate *Lodovico* weltring in his gore,
> Subtile *Francisco*, all of them shall bee
> Gaz'd at as Comets by Posteritie.[24]

The moral judgement against the machiavellian solitary was inherited from medieval drama, since the machiavellian had been anticipated long before Machiavelli by the Vice of the Morality plays, who was similarly isolated, dissembling, scheming and bent on breaking the bonds of community among men.[25] He was one of two traditional solitary characters in medieval drama: the other was God (or Christ), in the Mystery plays. Other characters might speak occasional soliloquies or hold the stage alone briefly, but only these two stood naturally and inherently apart. In accordance with Aristotle's sentiments, the solitary was either more or less than a man, and as such his moral status was clear and extreme.

Not until the sixteenth century does drama begin to present ordinary men as solitaries, and it is then that solitude becomes morally ambiguous. Clarence Boyer, in his book *The Villain as Hero in Elizabethan Tragedy* (1914)[26] singles out Marlowe as the first dramatist to present a morally ambiguous character, and considers Barabas to be the first villain-hero. But Boyer, oddly, does not point out the similarities between this heroic villain and Marlowe's other protagonists, often more clearly heroic than Barabas, while sharing some of his morally dubious characteristics. What Marlowe admires in Barabas, Tamburlaine and Faustus is a ruthless solitariness of spirit, an impassioned dedication to self and an acceptance of the consequence of living in conflict with the rest of the world. Just as prose writers on solitude admitted to its attractiveness while continuing to insist on sociability as a moral duty, so Marlowe portrays the attractive, or 'heroic', aspect of the solitary even where the moral judgement is finally pronounced against him.

Other dramatists (notably Chapman and Webster) followed Marlowe in demonstrating a fascination with the solitary while remaining uncertain about his moral status, although the admiration for the characteristics of the solitary is clear. Heroes and villains alike are seen as struggling against their society rather than at one with it. Alienation becomes more glamorous than participation, and where medieval characters were judged by their attitude to God or to the commonwealth, late sixteenth-century characters are defined by their attitudes to themselves. *The Mirror for Magistrates* (1559) is an example of a work in which the medieval perspective is clearly retained: the good and the evil are defined respectively as lovers of the commonwealth and as self-lovers. But those who fall to the forces of law and social order in the *Mirror* are the future heroes (and villains, of course) of the Elizabethan and Jacobean dramatists—proud, ambitious and self-seeking. Whereas the good in the *Mirror* embody duty and the necessities of law, accepting their place in a greater order, Elizabethan drama creates a new order, a new law, which binds the individual to himself alone. As Chapman writes:

> There is no danger to a man that knows
> What life and death is; there's not any law
> Exceeds his knowledge; neither is it lawful
> That he should stoop to any other law.
> He goes before them, and commands them all,
> That to himself is a law rational.[27]

Moral autonomy, individual freedom and a higher trust in the inward self than in the world outside the self are the familiar characteristics of the solitary.

Hand-in-hand with these attributes and the impulse to break free of the restrictions of the social bonds goes the aspiration towards self-definition. Only the Vice or a sinner in medieval drama would have given expression to the defiant self-assertion so characteristic of the protagonists of Renaissance drama. Such self-assertion is not limited to moral degenerates like Shakespeare's Richard III or Kyd's Lorenzo in Elizabethan and Jacobean drama, but is metamorphosed into the more morally ambiguous quality of truth to self in such characters as Chapman's Byron, with his proud rejection of authority: 'I will be mine own king' (*Byron's Conspiracy*, v. i. 138), or Webster's Duchess of Malfi, with her uncompromising endurance in the face of death: 'I am Duchess of Malfi still' (*Duchess of Malfi*, IV. ii. 142). The characters of Renaissance drama were not Everyman-types, representative of humanity in general, but individuals aware of their own individuality and proud of it. As such they were necessarily also inward characters, and the soliloquy became an increasingly important dramatic technique for the expression of the inner self. A drama which focused on protagonists who felt unexpressed, unfulfilled, or even betrayed, by the forms of their society needed a device whereby the private, unexpressed self of such an individual could be revealed, and soliloquy was developed to become this device. Where in earlier drama the function of soliloquy had been largely to provide exposition of the plot, it now became primarily a vehicle for the development of character, a medium of self-expression rather than narration.[28]

Perhaps the figure most strongly associated in medieval drama with soliloquy as a device for more than mere exposition was the Vice, who used soliloquy to cultivate a special relationship with the audience which emphasised his divided nature, his cultivation of a public self false to his private self. The increasing importance of soliloquy in Renaissance drama was symptomatic of a growing preoccupation with the notion of division, but the division portrayed was more complex. Involuntary as well as voluntary division was explored, and even voluntary division was not usually presented in such a way as to elicit simple moral condemnation. Dissembling was often admired for its very virtuosity, as for example in *The Alchemist* or *The Jew of Malta*, or justified as the response of a noble character to a corrupt society, as in *Hamlet* or *The Spanish Tragedy*.

Division in the individual could be vindicated as a natural response to a divided society, and these two aspects of the same theme are central to Elizabethan and Jacobean drama. Robert B. Heilman's description of the drama of this period as enacting the

conflict between 'imperative' and 'impulse' is based on essentially
the same principle as Bacon's theory concerning the division
inherent in all nature (discussed on pp. 35–6 above). Only the
terminology is different. Heilman's definition of 'imperative' and
'impulse' restates Bacon's distinction between existence as defined
by the larger context or as defined from within:

> . . . imperative is the overriding obligation, the discipline of self
> that cannot be rejected without penalty, whether it is felt as
> divine law, moral law, civil law, or in a less codified, but no less
> powerful way as tradition, duty, honor, 'principle', or 'voice of
> conscience.' Imperative reflects communal consciousness or
> higher law; impulse is open to challenge, judgment, or replace-
> ment in a way that imperative is not. Impulse originates in, is
> rooted in, or is identified with the individual personality; though
> the specific feelings that impel the individual may be of the widest
> occurrence in human kind, they are felt as a need, a satisfaction, a
> fulfillment, or an aggrandizement of the individual.[29]

Heilman is talking here purely about tragedy, describing the
conflict within the individual; but if impulse and imperative are
seen as the respective attributes of the individual and society viewed
externally they can also be applied to comedy. The conflict between
anti-social characters and the ideals of social harmony in comedy is
essentially the same as the conflict between the social and solitary
instincts within the tragic hero. Elizabethan drama, whatever its
genre, is based on the opposition between the social and the solitary
principles, and the moral ambiguity of the solitary life in this period
helps to account for the moral ambiguity of its isolated protagonists.

No dramatist of the time explores the implications of solitude and
the differing motivations and moral states of the solitary more fully
than Shakespeare. Given the preoccupation of his age with the idea
of solitude, and the contradictory and ambiguous nature of its
responses to the subject, it is necessary to study Shakespeare's work
in relation to this movement. An examination of the changing status
of the solitary in Shakespeare's writing provides the framework for
an examination of the much wider issue of Shakespeare's own values
and beliefs in a period of uncertainty and debate.

Part Two

4 'I am myself alone': *Richard III*

'Enter Richard, Duke of Gloucester, solus'. So the scene is set at the beginning of *Richard III*, the only one of Shakespeare's plays to open with a soliloquy by the main protagonist. Richard is isolated at the beginning of the play both by this stage direction (indicating his physical solitude on stage) and by the themes and images of his first soliloquy, which set up emblematically the solitary characteristics he will enact in the course of the play. An earlier soliloquy of Richard's in *3 Henry VI* has already shown him trapped between voluntary and involuntary types of isolation. There he self-consciously outlined the elements of wilful solitariness: ambition, egotism, ruthless disregard of other men, machiavellian skill in dissembling, absolute determination to have his own will. But more striking than these traditional aspects of the villain was the image of involuntary self-imprisonment in the same soliloquy, where he described himself as

> like one lost in a thorny wood,
> That rents the thorns and is rent with the thorns,
> Seeking a way and straying from the way;
> Not knowing how to find the open air,
> But toiling desperately to find it out.   (III. ii. 174–8)

The opening soliloquy of *Richard III* picks up another form of involuntary isolation, the physical deformity which sets him apart from others. The first person pronoun dominates the soliloquy with its implications of the voluntary isolation of egotism and self-love, but each time it is emphasised it is also linked with the unwilling isolation of deformity:

> But I—that am not shap'd for sportive tricks,
> Nor made to court an amorous looking-glass—

49

> I—that am rudely stamp'd, and want love's majesty
> To strut before a wanton ambling nymph—
> I—that am curtail'd of this fair proportion,
> Cheated of feature by dissembling nature,
> Deform'd, unfinish'd, sent before my time
> Into this breathing world scarce half made up,
> And that so lamely and unfashionable
> That dogs bark at me as I halt by them—
> Why, I, in this weak piping time of peace,
> Have no delight to pass away the time,
> Unless to spy my shadow in the sun
> And descant on mine own deformity.   (i. i. 14–27)

Richard's deformity figured prominently in historical accounts of his life. Holinshed, Halle and More, Shakespeare's sources, all describe it, seeing it as an omen of his later evil deeds. But for Shakespeare the deformity is more than an omen: it is an emblem of Richard's inherent unnaturalness, the external image of his inward corruption. It is a physical quality, setting him involuntarily apart from other men, which mirrors the inward solitude he cultivates voluntarily in keeping his thoughts to himself and refusing to acknowledge the social bonds which bind men to one another. No one knows Richard. He is known only to himself. When Buckingham, speaking of the forthcoming coronation of Richard, asks:

> Who knows the Lord Protector's mind herein?
> Who is most inward with the noble Duke?
>
>   (iii. iv. 8–9)

the Bishop of Ely replies:

> Your Grace, we think, should soonest know his mind,   (10)

and Buckingham denies any such 'inwardness' with Richard:

> We know each other's faces; for our hearts,
> He knows no more of mine than I of yours;
> Or I of his, my lord, than you of mine,   (11–13)

turning immediately to someone else:

Lord Hastings, you and he are near in love.   (14)

Hastings too, of course, denies knowing any more of Richard than
his surface. The full irony of this universal sense of Richard as
unknown to any, close to no man, becomes clear in the next scene
when Richard, on being presented with Hastings' head, talks as
though they had been truly intimate:

> So dear I lov'd the man that I must weep.
> I took him for the plainest harmless creature
> That breath'd upon the earth a Christian;
> Made him my book, wherein my soul recorded
> The history of all her secret thoughts.   (III. v. 24–8)

The reason no one knows Richard is that he consciously cultivates
a division between face and heart, deliberately keeping his inner self
apart from the calculated public face he presents to the world.[1] The
irony is stressed throughout Act III, Scene iv, where all admit to
finding Richard distant and unfathomable to each of them
individually, yet Hastings, even while recognising that he knows
only the facade, seems to think it truly represents Richard's heart:

> I think there's never a man in Christendom
> Can lesser hide his love or hate than he;
> For by his face straight shall you know his heart.
>   (III. iv. 53–5)

The audience knows that Richard is false, not because those around
him perceive it, but because he himself has an openly confessional
relationship with the audience inherited from the Vice of the
Morality plays, a relationship which also sets him structurally apart
from other characters in the play, rather as though he is standing
outside the play watching it as if it were a play-within-a-play.
   This self-conscious movement between play and audience is
made explicit from the first soliloquy:

> I am determined to prove a villain . . .
> As I am subtle, false, and treacherous . . .
> Dive, thoughts, down to my soul. Here Clarence comes.
>   (I. i. 30, 37, 41)

Soliloquies and asides become a characteristic mode of speech, enabling Richard to declare his techniques openly:

> I clothe my naked villainy
> With odd old ends stol'n forth of holy writ,
> And seem a saint when most I play the devil.
>
> (I. iii. 336–8)

He even acknowledges his literary ancestry in a way that sets him further beyond the fiction of the play:

> Thus, like the formal vice, Iniquity,
> I moralize two meanings in one word.   (III. i. 82–3)

Richard's structural isolation becomes an image of his social and moral isolation; just as he refuses to become fully committed to the artifice of the play, but stands outside it as a mocking observer, so he refuses to commit himself to humanity and its laws, but stands outside the framework of traditional values as a moral and social outlaw. Anne's first speech on meeting Richard, before he has manipulated her responses out of their natural direction, expresses her sense that Richard is somehow outside humanity, outside the natural order:

> Foul devil, for God's sake, hence and trouble us not...
> Dead Henry's wounds
> Open their congeal'd mouths and bleed afresh.
> Blush, blush, thou lump of foul deformity,
> For 'tis thy presence that exhales this blood
> From cold and empty veins where no blood dwells;
> Thy deeds inhuman and unnatural
> Provokes this deluge most unnatural...
> Villain, thou knowest nor law of God nor man:
> No beast so fierce but knows some touch of pity.
>
> (I. ii. 50, 55–61, 70–1)

Richard gives her the typically riddling reply of the Vice:

> But I know none, and therefore am no beast   (72)

and she responds bitterly:

> O wonderful, when devils tell the truth!   (73)

She recognises that Richard's deformity is a mark of his inhumanity, his unlikeness to natural man. The imagery she uses to refer to him throughout this speech moves between devil and beast, and this is true of other characters' references to Richard too. The devil imagery links him with the Vice, as we have seen; the beast imagery harks back to Aristotle's condemnation of the solitary as unnatural, 'either a beast or a god' (p. 4 above).

Yet Richard's isolation from common humanity clearly suggests something of the superhuman as well as the subhuman. His deformity does not simply mark out his limitations, but also draws attention to his remarkable ability to overcome his limitations. Even though he carries the mark of inhumanity in his physical shape, he can bewitch his audience into overlooking what is before their eyes and submitting to his deceptive charisma. The last scenes of the play taunt the audience with this alternation between the superhuman and the subhuman. Catesby's wonder in the face of Richard's actions at Bosworth: 'The King enacts more wonders than a man' (v. iv. 2) gives place to Richmond's affirmation in the next scene: 'The day is ours, the bloody dog is dead' (v. v. 2).

Richard's charms do not work on all the members of his audience within the play, however, and the women in the play repeatedly curse his unnaturalness and see his physical deformity as a mark of a mode of existence outside humanity. Only Anne is induced to change her mind. Margaret maintains the position from which Anne starts, and the images of devil and beast dominate her abuse of Richard:

> Thou elvish-mark'd, abortive, rooting hog,
> Thou that wast seal'd in thy nativity
> The slave of nature and the son of hell,
> Thou slander of thy heavy mother's womb,
> Thou loathed issue of thy father's loins.
>
>   (i. iii. 228–32)

Even Richard's mother condemns his unnaturalness:

Thou cam'st on earth to make the earth my hell.
A grievous burden was thy birth to me ...
What comfortable hour canst thou name
That ever grac'd me with thy company?
                                    (IV. iv. 166–7, 173–4)

and adds her curse to Margaret's.

Richard wilfully rejects the bonds of kinship and fellowship. His aspiration towards absolute and uncompromising self-definition and self-sufficiency is made clear even in *3 Henry VI*:

I have no brother, I am like no brother;
And this word 'love', which greybeards call divine,
Be resident in men like one another,
And not in me! I am myself alone.   (v. vi. 80–3)

And this circular, solipsistic condition finds an image in the structure of *Richard III*, which itself forms a circle around Richard in the placing of similar statements of self-enclosure at the beginning and end of the play:

I ...
Have no delight to pass away the time,
Unless to spy my shadow in the sun
And descant on mine own deformity   (I. i. 24–7)

Richard loves Richard; that is, I am I.   (v. iii. 183)

Even the grammar forms imitative circles in this last utterance, enclosing the verbs, which denote Richard's action and being, within the names of the self, which mark the limits of his existence and define the space which contains his action and being. The statements at the end of *3 Henry VI* and at the end of *Richard III* also echo two of God's statements (already cited on pp. 9 and 29 above): 'It is not good that the man should be himself alone' and 'I AM THAT I AM'.[2] As such they embody simultaneously the heroic and the blasphemous in Richard, formulating the challenge to God while also drawing attention to the moral depravity inherent in such a challenge, however attractive it may be in amoral terms.

The phrase 'myself myself', pervasive in Richard's speech, is a similar expression of his aspiration towards inhuman self-containment and his cultivation of a double self, one which is solitary and one which deceives others.[3] This speech-pattern, in which the two elements occur sometimes in sequence and sometimes separated, begins after Richard's first triumph of dissembling, a triumph which also feeds his self-love: the wooing of Anne. Because Richard manages to twist Anne into finding 'Myself to be a marv'llous proper man' (I. ii. 254), he finds himself to be 'crept in favour with myself' (258) and resolves to buy a mirror, traditionally emblematic of self-love:

> Shine out, fair sun, till I have bought a glass,
> That I may see my shadow as I pass.   (262–3)

This resolve, however mockingly intended, confirms Richard's doubleness as well as his self-love, since the mirror reflects a second image of the self, and echoes too his profession of love for his own shadow in the first soliloquy.

The 'myself myself' pattern is at its most prominent again in the second wooing scene, where Richard tries to re-enact his initial triumph of dissembling over Anne by persuading Elizabeth to let him marry her daughter. But this scene shows Richard losing control over his doubleness and proving himself unable to deceive Elizabeth. This is partly demonstrated in the way Elizabeth takes up the challenge of this very verbal pattern, which has signalled his self-control, and manipulates it to his disadvantage, so that it comes instead to represent his confusion and loss of control. His last expression of the phrase in this scene is symptomatic of his failure: 'Myself myself confound!' (IV. iv. 399), whereas Elizabeth's last employment of it is a question which formulates her rebellion against Richard's dissembling: 'Shall I forget myself to be myself?' (420). The question is a masterpiece of ambiguity which rivals Richard's own riddling. Richard (or the audience) can take it as a rhetorical expression of amazement at her own ability to be persuaded by Richard; or it can be seen as conscious dissembling on her part, which is to be interpreted in the first way by Richard, but to be perceived by the audience as a mockery of Richard's *self*-deceit in imagining he could dupe her in this way. The second alternative, given Elizabeth's ability to turn Richard's verbal tricks against him throughout the scene, seems the more appropriate.

This interpretation is appropriate too if the scene is viewed as a stage in Richard's downfall and in the disruption of his verbal control over his voluntary self-division. The climax of this movement is achieved in Richard's final soliloquy, where ghosts, dreams and conscience have fully usurped Richard's self-control, and the involuntary solitude and division of this state of mind mock the voluntary solitude and division which he gloried in in his first soliloquies. The 'myself myself' pattern now takes the form of questions, showing Richard's present mood of self-doubt and fear by contrast with his previous absolute and self-assured statements:

> Is there a murderer here? No—yes, I am.
> Then fly. What, from myself? Great reason why—
> Lest I revenge. What, myself upon myself!
> Alack, I love myself. Wherefore? For any good
> That I myself have done unto myself?
> O, no! Alas, I rather hate myself
> For hateful deeds committed by myself! . . .
> I shall despair. There is no creature loves me;
> And if I die no soul will pity me:
> And wherefore should they, since that I myself
> Find in myself no pity to myself?
>
> (v. iii. 184–90, 200–3)

Richard at last sees that his severing of all bonds with other men, his wilful isolation of himself, has destroyed him. Having rejected the love of others in favour of self-love, he now finds that he cannot even love himself any longer and yearns for love or pity from another.

It is not only the individual who suffers as a result of his withdrawal from social commitment, but society as a whole. If individual withdrawal becomes widespread, society necessarily disintegrates; and fear of such disintegration was often expressed in Shakespeare's time. There is no greater threat to the social order than the anarchic individualist, like Richard.

> Whom neither dread of God, that devils bindes,
> Nor lawes of men, that common weales containe,
> Nor bands of nature, that wilde beastes restraine,
> Can keepe from outrage, and from doing wrong,[4]

particularly when such a man aspires to the throne of the kingdom. The familiar Elizabethan prophecies of the chaos of civil war that will ensue out of self-love and denial of social responsibility are

echoed twice in *Richard III*, first in the Duchess of York's lament for
the division within her family, whose members,

> themselves the conquerors
> Make war upon themselves—brother to brother,
> Blood to blood, self against self,   (II. iv. 61–3)

and again in Richmond's final summary of events:

> England hath long been mad, and scarr'd herself;
> The brother blindly shed the brother's blood,
> The father rashly slaughter'd his own son,
> The son, compell'd, been butcher to the sire;
> All this divided York and Lancaster,
> Divided in their dire division.[5]   (v. v. 23–8)

Richard knows that his cultivation of division within himself
produces division in the world around him; he acknowledges that he
is 'like to a chaos' (*3H6*, III. ii. 161). The machiavel undercuts the
basis of social harmony, rooted in trust and communication
between men, by inculcating the fear in men that others are double
and false, and present mere shows of truth. Richard willingly
corrupts the next generation with this distrust, telling the young
Prince of Wales:

> Sweet Prince, the untainted virtue of your years
> Hath not yet div'd into the world's deceit;
> Nor more can you distinguish of a man
> Than of his outward show; which, God He knows,
> Seldom or never jumpeth with the heart.   (III. i. 7–11)

It is Richard, however, not society, that is destroyed in this play,
because Richard does not accept his own humanity, and therefore
does not fully know himself. He thinks he can control the
relationship between his private and public selves, thinks he can be
wholly self-sufficient and self-absorbed, unfettered by any ties of
relationship. In this sense he thinks he is unlike other men, not
bound by the limitations of natural man. But, despite the fact that
others view him as subhuman throughout the play, while he is
aspiring to be superhuman, the end of the play reveals him to be
finally constrained by the limitations of his own humanity. He loses

his control over his wilful self-division and comes to regret his choice
of total self-dedication to the exclusion of all relationship. According
to Anne, he has had bad dreams from the very beginning, even
when his control seemed absolute:

> For never yet one hour in his bed
> Did I enjoy the golden dew of sleep,
> But with his timorous dreams was still awak'd;
>
> (IV. i. 83–5)

and Richard himself reveals that he has been long tormented by
ambiguous prophecies (IV. ii. 99–111). Throughout the play, then,
the impossibility of his aspiration to transcend his humanity has
thrust itself upon him, so that the final victory over him of the moral
laws he has tried to reject is the fulfilment of a doubt which has
always underlain even his most assured performances.

The changing contexts of the image of the glass contribute too to
reveal the transformation of his inhumanly willed solitude into an
all too human imprisonment within the torments of his own soul.
The early associations of glass and shadow with Richard's love of his
own degradation and his self-satisfied control over his own doubleness change as the images move subtly out of these contexts of
studied reflection into those of unsolicited reflections and shadows,
manifested through nightmare and conscience. The shadows of
himself which Richard deliberately and mockingly summoned in
Act I give way to the more potent shadows of an unacknowledged
self, and Richard's end is a climactic victory for these second
shadows over the first. As Richard says on the eve of Bosworth:

> By the apostle Paul, shadows to-night
> Have struck more terror to the soul of Richard
> Than can the substance of ten thousand soldiers.
>
> (V. iii. 216–18)

Richard's death is prefigured by an all-enveloping shadow, an
unnatural refusal of the sun to shine, at least within his sphere of
vision (one of Shakespeare's more conspicuous departures from
Holinshed). Another structural pattern is thus formed to ridicule
Richard's self-consuming solipsism: Richard's challenge to the sun
to shine so that he could see his own shadow in Act I is answered in

Act v by mockery, as the sun refuses to shine for him on the day of his death.

The structural circles perform a double function in this play: not only do they describe Richard's confinement within the circle of his own self, they also describe the circle of society which encloses him against his will and which he attempts to deny. Richard stands apart from the structure of the play at the beginning, a mocking showman observing the antics of his puppets, but the final impossibility of such isolation is demonstrated through the gradual closing in of the larger structure on Richard until he is totally subsumed within it by his death, the final overturning of his individual values by the moral laws of society. In retrospect it can be seen that this closing in was foreshadowed even in the early scenes, where Richard seemed set apart.[6] His own downfall is repeatedly anticipated in that of others; the dreams of death described in such detail by Clarence and Stanley prefigure Anne's revelation that Richard himself is tormented by such dreams; the pangs of conscience experienced by Clarence's murderers anticipate the way in which conscience overtakes Richard at last. Even the mirror image, Richard's own image of self-congratulation, is turned against him by his mother before he himself sees its brittleness: compared with his brothers, 'two mirrors' of their father, Richard, she says, is a 'false glass' (II. ii. 51, 53). Once Richard is King, he begins to use the word 'glass' in a changed sense, which emphasises brittleness in place of the capacity for reflection:

> I must be married to my brother's daughter,
> Or else my kingdom stands on brittle glass.
>
> (IV. ii. 62–3)

Richard's fight to sever himself from all social laws and values, his attempt to become a self-defining whole in himself, rather than simply a part in the social whole, can be seen in this play through the struggle of Richard as character to break out of the laws and framework of the play. He refuses to confine himself to the limits of the play by expressing himself in communion with other characters, but instead insists on dissembling within the play and restricting the communication of his true self to the soliloquies and asides through which he develops a special relationship with the audience. He insists on forming his own circles and laying down his own terms instead of accommodating himself to the wider circles of society, humanity and the play itself. In these respects Richard elicits an awe akin to admiration and displays a defiance which is as heroic as it is villainous.

But Shakespeare undercuts Richard's heroic aspect by making his gestures finally futile. Richard's solitude does not achieve the status it seeks, of pure self-referentiality. It is judged from outside by the values of the framework it pretends to reject, and seen as an aberration from norms which impose themselves on it by sheer force. The individualist at last meets the death he has brought on himself by having cut himself off from society, and is shown to be weaker than those social values he deludes himself into thinking he can reject. The play thus offers an essentially medieval perspective, resolutely preventing the aspiring solitary from creating his own laws and portraying him as subject to society whatever his pretensions. As the play moves towards its close, the focus widens, moving away from the solitary individual towards the re-ordering society, which has the last word and the final victory over Richard. With the anarchic solitary dead, the kingdom can look forward again to order and harmony. In place of the division and disorder created by Richard, Richmond and Elizabeth enact the social ideal of concord in marrying, and the play ends with Richmond illustrating his affirmation of traditional social values by concentrating primarily not on his individual desires, but on the common good and on God's will for society as a whole:

> Now civil wounds are stopp'd, peace lives again—
> That she may long live here, God say amen!
>
> (V. V. 40–1)

5 'This prison where I live': *Richard II*

Richard III was a condemnation of one solitary individual: *Richard II* expands this single focus into a multiple perspective which makes simple condemnation impossible. The play explores three different kinds of solitude: the solitudes inherent in the natures of Richard, Bolingbroke and of kingship itself. Both Richard and Bolingbroke, as well as possessing characteristics of solitude peculiar to themselves, participate in this third, more abstract kind of solitude, which is one that Shakespeare explores in several plays. He sees the king as set apart from other men by his position, but simultaneously, as king, symbolically representative of other men. The king is both human and superhuman, possessing, according to medieval theory, two bodies, the first mortal, the body of the particular king at any one time, the second immortal, passing from king to king, the body of the public role.[1] The king was thus the image of God as well as of man: as head of the kingdom, he was a symbol of God on earth and of the divine potential within man, a mediating vehicle between the levels of human and divine through which God could reveal himself on earth and men could find fulfilment, by transferring their potential imaginatively to the person of the king, who 'is in act what everyman is only in potency'.[2]

Paradoxically, these divisions and dualities inherent in kingship were supposed to contribute to an image not of archetypal division, but of archetypal unity. The king ought to be an emblem of harmony and reconciliation, both on a social and on a moral level, and perhaps also within the individual self, as Philip Edwards has suggested, 'as a metaphor for a harmony of the personality, the unity of being and doing when private person and public office are one'.[3] In fact, however, the particular king may feel set apart from other men not only by his divine body, and his singularity in this respect, but by the fact that he is symbolically representative of mankind, and hence unlike mere men in this respect too. The extent to which the king is unlike other men and set apart from them was magnified from early Tudor times onwards for political reasons, to safeguard the king against rebellion or having to relinquish more power to the people. King James's advice to his son contains a reminder of the union of human and divine within the king when he warns him of his double obligation towards man and God 'first, for that he made you a man, and next, for that he made you a little God to sit on his Throne, & rule over other men';[4] but the phrase 'a little God' suggests the inflation of this half of the duality, which distanced the king from the world of men, and hence also from the ideal unity in balance.

Shakespeare's Richard II is very far from being an ideal king, and stands as an emblem not of unity but of division. Ironically, his sense of self-division arises out of his inflation of the divine element in kingship, and thus out of his remoteness from ordinary humanity, yet in being so conscious of self-division he also becomes representative of many of the ordinary men of Shakespeare's time, who were torn also by different forms of self-division. Richard's self-division, however, arises primarily out of his inability to reconcile his private, human nature with his responsibility towards a theoretical ideal, and he feels a separation between his inner self and his role. His insecurity is demonstrated by his constant need to remind others of the sacred inviolability and divine anointment of a king and by his obsession with death, which marks the ultimate division of the two bodies. His inadequacy as king is also unconsciously revealed in his use of the analogy between himself and Christ. This was an analogy frequently used by medieval political theorists to explain the union of a divine and a human body in the king; but all Richard's references are to Christ's mortal body, which embodies the human element, and never to his resurrected body, the proof of his divinity. Richard always parallels himself with the betrayed or suffering Christ, and by limiting Christ in this way he betrays his own limitations and his inability to transcend his devotion to the private self, despite his preoccupation with his imagined divinity.

Richard enacts the chasm between private and public which signifies the failure to achieve ideal kingship. His preoccupation with his own private world results in his political downfall, and that in turn destroys his private world, which is left meaningless, based as it was upon images of his ideal public self. Though he appears to be involved in the world outside himself, he fails to understand its

objective relevance because he transposes it into his private
terminology and forces it to become part of his inner world. On his
return from Ireland, for example, his love for his kingdom is seen to
be private and emotional, instead of politically responsible:

> I weep for joy
> To stand upon my kingdom once again.
> Dear earth, I do salute thee with my hand,
> Though rebels wound thee with their horses' hoofs.
> As a long-parted mother with her child
> Plays fondly with her tears and smiles in meeting,
> So weeping-smiling greet I thee, my earth,
> And do thee favours with my royal hands.
>
> (III. ii. 4–11)

This expresses a closed, self-indulgent and sentimental relationship
with England seen as an ideal image, separate from its inhabitants
(the rebels), and is notable for the absence of any attempt to
understand or manage the causes of the rebels' discontent.

Division between role and self is inherent in the texture of
Richard's speech: he repeatedly calls himself 'the King' and talks
about himself in the third person, particularly once his status as king
is threatened. Later in the scene which begins with the return from
Ireland, Richard makes the disparateness between 'person' and
'office' quite explicit by addressing one with the other, making his
monologue resemble dialogue:

> I had forgot myself; am I not King?
> Awake, thou coward majesty! thou sleepest. (83–4)

The unacceptability of this sense of division can be measured by
direct comparison with one statement of medieval theory concerning the king:

> . . . he has not a Body natural distinct and divided by itself from
> the Office and Dignity royal, but a Body natural and a Body
> politic together indivisible; and these two Bodies are incorpo-
> rated in one Person, and make one Body and not divers.[5]

The same sense of division pervades the next scene too, where the
role of kingship is reduced to a mere name:

> O, that I were as great
> As is my grief, or lesser than my name!
> Or that I could forget what I have been!
> Or not remember what I must be now!
>
> (III. iii. 136–9)

He uses the name of King like an incantation to try to summon up integrity of being:

> What must the King do now? Must he submit?
> The King shall do it. Must he be depos'd?
> The King shall be contented,   (143–5)

but the irony of his position is clear. He chooses the moment in which he is renouncing his kingship to summon himself to behave like a king, and merely restates the distance between himself and the ideal king by giving expression to such an incongruity. Richard himself implicitly acknowledges the absurdity by immediately contradicting the role of king with a desire for the totally private and inward life of a hermit:

> Must he lose
> The name of king? A God's name, let it go.
> I'll give my jewels for a set of beads,
> My gorgeous palace for a hermitage.   (145–8)

The appeal of such a life lies in its remoteness from the possibility of a division between private and public self. The hermit has no public life; his inner life is his role.

Richard's longing for the hermit's life is a direct expression of the disparity between his public duty and his individual desire and closely echoes those Elizabethan courtiers, like Essex and Ralegh, who expressed their longing for a life of solitude in lyrics while remaining in public life. But if Richard is torn between a private longing for solitude and a public duty to the state, Bolingbroke is at the opposite extreme, longing for the power and public position Richard has, but driven unwillingly into the solitude of exile. Dissimilar as they seem, however, in relation to solitude of time and place, both share a solitude of mind. They are both disengaged from any real concern for the public good, both preoccupied with themselves and their individual desires more than with any sense of duty, and both self-divided. Richard isolates himself by his attempt to escape from responsibility and retreat into the safety of the inner world; Bolingbroke, like Richard III, isolates himself by his dissembling, his masking of his inner motivations behind a false show in order to work his way into a position of power. Both Richard and Bolingbroke play roles in public.

Richard demonstrates a love of the show of kingship, the ceremonial and self-dramatisation. He cultivates all those rituals and ceremonies which emphasise the aloofness and separateness of the king. The separation of the two bodies in him is again confirmed by his association of his kingship with externals, mere hollow show, and of his sincere self with privacy. The king is of course particularly vulnerable to the feeling that he is merely role-playing,[6] but it is a feeling shared by more than kings, particularly in Shakespeare's time. Elizabethans, as they became increasingly preoccupied by the inner self, increasingly 'self-conscious', became correspondingly tormented by the fear that the self-consciousness of any action somehow negated its sincerity. The image of the world as a stage dominates the literature of this period, and the link between the preoccupation with sincerity and the flourishing of the theatre has been suggested by Lionel Trilling in *Sincerity and Authenticity* (2nd ed., Oxford, 1974). Although kingship is a classic mode of expressing the division between self and role, Richard is not the only self-conscious actor in the play. Bolingbroke, even before he becomes king, is a more skilful actor than Richard. Immediately after his exile is pronounced, Richard describes

> his courtship to the common people;
> How he did seem to dive into their hearts
> With humble and familiar courtesy;
> What reverence he did throw away on slaves,
> Wooing poor craftsmen with the craft of smiles.
>
> (I. iv. 24–8)

York uses a theatrical image to describe Richard's reception by the common people as compared with Bolingbroke's, which clearly points to Bolingbroke as the more subtle actor:

> As in a theatre the eyes of men
> After a well-grac'd actor leaves the stage
> Are idly bent on him that enters next,

> Thinking his prattle to be tedious;
> Even so, or with much more contempt, men's eyes
> Did scowl on gentle Richard.   (v. ii. 23–8)

But as Bolingbroke is a better actor than Richard, so his sense of the chasm between private and public is even more pronounced than Richard's. When Richard voices the feeling that he is no more than a man:

>   you have but mistook me all this while.
> I live with bread like you, feel want,
> Taste grief, need friends; subjected thus,
> How can you say to me I am a king?   (iii. ii. 174–7)

he can be at least partly excused by the fact that his kingship is threatened. Bolingbroke feels this vulnerability even before he is king, since he cannot have even the security of birthright that Richard has, and this doubt intensifies once he becomes king. He is a usurper, shown tormented by guilt in *1 Henry IV*, and he passes on his guilt even to Henry v, who continues to view kingship as a garment, a detachable robe covering a mere man. Although Henry v is politically a better king than Richard ii, he is even further from being able to unite the two bodies of kingship in accordance with the medieval ideal.

The chasm that exists for both Richard and Bolingbroke between their true selves and society is exemplified in their use of language. Neither uses words as simple counters for making public private truth; both demonstrate their respective forms of isolation in their attitudes to language. Bolingbroke's secretiveness and his lack of commitment to the common good are expressed in his dislike of language, the element of communication. When he does speak it is not to externalise any inward truth, but to announce some public gesture. His words are inseparably linked with deeds from the first scene:

>   what I speak
> My body shall make good upon this earth   (i. i. 36–7)

> With a foul traitor's name stuff I thy throat;
> And wish—so please my sovereign—ere I move,
> What my tongue speaks, my right drawn sword may prove
>   (44–6)

Look what I speak, my life shall prove it true—   (87)

Besides, I say and will in battle prove   (92)

Further I say, and further will maintain
Upon his bad life to make all this good . . .   (98–9)

None of these words brings us any closer to the inner man. Words
such as these mask the self as effectively as actions can. And there is
also the sense that it is a point of honour with Bolingbroke to link his
words with action, thereby expressing his contempt for those who
play with words for their own sake, or as a substitute for action, like
Richard. When he receives the sentence of banishment, his father
pleads with him for a few words of emotion, from within himself:

O, to what purpose dost thou hoard thy words,
That thou returnest no greeting to thy friends?
                                          (I. iii. 253–4)

and Bolingbroke maintains his closed quality:

I have too few to take my leave of you,
When the tongue's office should be prodigal
To breathe the abundant dolour of the heart.   (255–7)

Aumerle mocks this taciturnity to Richard in describing how
Bolingbroke went into banishment:

K. Rich. What said our cousin when you parted with him?
Aum. 'Farewell.'   (I. iv. 10–11)

Bolingbroke, however, is equally capable of mocking Richard's
lavishness with words, and when Richard takes four years off his
sentence of exile, Bolingbroke comments bitterly:

How long a time lies in one little word!
Four lagging winters and four wanton springs
End in a word: such is the breath of Kings.
                                          (I. iii. 213–15)

He despises Richard for making language a substitute for action.
Indeed, a comparison of Richard's behaviour in the first scene of the

play with Bolingbroke's unremitting linking of words with action parades the difference between them. Richards extracts every possible opportunity for verbal ceremonial out of the occasion, only to terminate the scene before any action can take place, postponing the duel until another occasion, when he again stops the proceedings before the action starts and ends them with words in his sentences of banishment. His responses to grief and to leave-taking may be similarly compared with Bolingbroke's. When Richard hears of the deaths of Bushy, Green and Wiltshire, his first need is to talk:

> Let's talk of graves, of worms, and epitaphs;
> Make dust our paper, and with rainy eyes
> Write sorrow on the bosom of the earth.
> Let's choose executors and talk of wills . . .
> For God's sake let us sit upon the ground
> And tell sad stories of the death of kings,
>
> (III. ii. 145–8, 155–6)

and Carlisle remarks wrily:

> My lord, wise men ne'er sit and wail their woes,
> But presently prevent the ways to wail.   (178–9)

Richard's response to Bolingbroke's return is a grim reminder of Bolingbroke's comment on the power of Richard's words when he reduced Bolingbroke's sentence of exile:

> O God, O God! that e'er this tongue of mine
> That laid the sentence of dread banishment
> On yon proud man should take it off again
> With words of sooth!   (III. iii. 133–6)

Characteristically too, he extends his lament for another thirty lines or so, until he sees his own absurdity:

> Well, well, I see
> I talk but idly, and you laugh at me.   (170–1)

Taking leave of Isabella to go to prison, he is concerned that his story should be told after him, and asks Isabella:

Tell thou the lamentable tale of me,
And send the hearers weeping to their beds.   (v.i. 44–5)

Their parting takes up a whole scene, and Richard's last words are ironically reminiscent of Bolingbroke's refusal to be 'prodigal' of tongue:

We make woe wanton with this fond delay.
Once more, adieu; the rest let sorrow say.   (101–2)

Yet Richard is as isolated in his stream of words as Bolingbroke is in his silence. All the most beautiful speeches in the play are circling, self-regarding meditations of Richard's, mere excrescences in terms of plot. They confirm Richard's imprisonment in his own self-love; they are the speeches of 'a man going about his mind's engrossing business in a solitude of its own making'.[7] Everything Richard sees in the world outside him becomes transformed into a part of his private world. His preoccupation with self makes him refer everything outside himself to his own inner world and distorts his vision. To some extent, of course, subjectivity is a natural and inevitable condition of perception. As Bacon says,

. . . the mind of man is far from the nature of a clear and equal glass, wherein the beams of things should reflect according to their true incidence; nay, it is rather like an enchanted glass, full of superstition and imposture, if it be not delivered and reduced.[8]

Shakespeare shows his own awareness of the natural differences in perception among different individuals: both Hamlet and Antony use the formation of shapes by clouds as an example of the way the same object can be variously perceived.[9] But Richard's subjectivity is the exaggerated subjectivity of the solitary. Although Bacon uses the image of the glass to explain the natural subjectivity of perception, he nevertheless sees in Narcissus, who is obsessed with his own reflection, a type of the man whose vision is so dominated by images of the self that he can see nothing else (see p. 29 above). Richard is such a Narcissus type, as his need of a real mirror at a point of crisis demonstrates.

The mirror is a recurrent image in Shakespeare's portrayal of the solitary, inward-looking self. We have already seen the way he uses it to highlight the changing self-awareness of Richard III, extending its traditional associations with vanity and self-love[10] to encompass a wide range of aspects of the self. The versatility of the mirror as an image for different qualities in the self mimics the very variety and fickleness of the self: all its qualities, its smoothness, its superficiality, its facility, its brittleness, not to mention its capacity for reflection, are exploited. The ambiguity of its more familiar sixteenth-century synonym, 'glass', may begin to suggest something of its range and complexity as an image. Glass can be looked through, at what lies beyond, or into, that is back, at one's own image. It can thus suggest a movement beyond the surface, or between surfaces, a movement outward beyond the confines of the self or inward into the self, a linear or a circular movement. It can represent the self-awareness, or self-division, of the self, by presenting it as two, observer and observed. It can embody perception or the subjectivity of perception. It can express the attainment of new knowledge, or the way in which all apparently new knowledge returns to the same ancient knowledge. And it can offer in its smoothness a perfect image of wholeness, or, by shattering, an image of multiplicity or fragmentation.

Richard asks for a mirror at a point where the image of self he has had all his life is being questioned. He is at his most subjective here, yet simultaneously aware and critical of his own subjectivity. His kingship, which up to now has been a key element in his sense of his own identity, is about to be taken from him by a mere act of will on the part of another man, and he must somehow accommodate his sense of self to this loss of role. Losing the role he had thought was permanent forces him to try to identify himself with temporary, arbitrary roles; in this instance, the grief which is the immediate replacement for his usurped kingship. He looks in the glass for confirmation that he is real and convincing in the role of grief, hoping to see a visual image dominated by grief, but the glass shows him only the same division between private and public selves which has tormented him as king, reflecting only a superficial image which conveys nothing of the inner world. The mirror, traditionally supposed to aid self-knowledge, fulfils this function for Richard not by presenting him with a true image of his inner self, but by forcing him to reject its image as false.[11] The truth he learns through rejecting this false image concerns his own facility in assuming false images, and the fragility of such illusions. The mirror, in presenting a false image, deludes him in the same way as his flatterers have deluded him and as he has deluded himself; and in allowing itself to be so easily smashed, it shows him the brittleness of his own former image. He thought himself inviolable and invincible as king, but falling so far short of ideal kingship and failing to unite the two bodies of kingship in perfect, seamless wholeness as he did, he was in fact as brittle as the glass that enacts his fall. Smashing the glass is simultaneously an act of strength, since Richard thus rejects flattery, self-delusion and facile role-playing, and an enactment of brittleness, as Richard himself acknowledges:

> A brittle glory shineth in this face;
> As brittle as the glory is the face.   (IV. i. 287–8)

The statement is reminiscent of Richard III's recognition of the brittleness of his state (p. 59 above), but for Richard the recognition goes deeper, embracing the fragility of identity and kingship alike, not simply of a temporary political situation. The brittleness of the self is simply made more poignant by the irony that this particular self has thought itself sacred and invulnerable by reason of its kingship, whereas it is as subject to delusion, self-division and death as any other. As Donne says: 'A glass is not the less brittle, because a king's face is represented in it; nor a king the less brittle, because God is represented in him.'[12]

The smashing of the glass seems even more ironic when one considers the image Richard is rejecting in smashing (that of a self which appears other than it is, a mere facade) alongside the gesture of smashing, which is purely histrionic. Richard's self-knowledge does not really change him: in smashing the multiple self and its love of dramatisation he is actually re-enacting these same characteristics. Richard moralises on the gesture, and Bolingbroke voices his scepticism:

> *K. Rich.* Mark, silent king, the moral of this sport—
>   How soon my sorrow hath destroy'd my face.
> *Bol.* The shadow of your sorrow hath destroy'd
>   The shadow of your face.   (290–3)

Bolingbroke exposes the self-dramatisation of the gesture by questioning its reality, suggesting that it is all mere playing with shadows. The potentially contradictory relation of the glass to truth allows it to act as an image for the contradictory ways in which Richard and Bolingbroke perceive the same event. The glass can stand either as an archetypal ideal, a perfect representation of truth, or as a cheap pretence, or falsehood, by virtue of the fact that it *is* only a representation, a mere imitation, or even a distortion of truth. 'Shadow' was often used in Shakespeare's time as a synonym for 'reflection', and both these words can carry overtones of unreality and insubstantiality. To Bolingbroke, Richard's behaviour is unreal, mere playing with surfaces, but to Richard, shadows offer a way of reaching truth through the very recognition of their inadequacy:

> The shadow of my sorrow? Ha! let's see.
> 'Tis very true: my grief lies all within;
> And these external manner of laments
> Are merely shadows to the unseen grief
> That swells with silence in the tortur'd soul.   (294–8)

To Bolingbroke, shadows are opposed to reality, but to Richard they are an aspect of its multiplicity, an instance of the fickle relation between internal and external reality. The separation between private and public reality for Richard II means that for him, as for Richard III, 'shadows' can come to embody a paradox which torments him: he is preoccupied by the shadows of the inner life to the point where the inner world seems more real than the outer, so that the outer world, the public roles and the surfaces of things, seem to be shadows in his scale of the real.

The disruption of public, social life by self-absorption, as expressed through the imagery of shadow and reflection, is finally as self-consuming and sterile for Richard II as it was for Richard III. Fragmentation within, like the fragment of the mirror in Hans Andersen's *The Snow Queen*, distorts the vision so that the world outside the self seems fragmented too. The glazed eye of sorrow, a variation on the mirror image, sees in the world an image of its own inner fragmentation:

> Each substance of a grief hath twenty shadows,
> Which shows like grief itself, but is not so;
> For sorrow's eye, glazed with blinding tears,
> Divides one thing entire to many objects,
> Like perspectives which, rightly gaz'd upon,
> Show nothing but confusion—ey'd awry,
> Distinguish form.   (II. ii. 14–20)

But the world outside does not merely seem fragmented; it *is* fragmented, divided, as in *Richard III*, by analogy with the self-division of the individual. Division within the individual, particularly the head of the body politic, produces social division, seen at its most extreme in civil war. The garden scene, Act III, Scene iv, which is, like the mirror scene, one of Shakespeare's additions to his source material, makes explicit the analogy between disorder in the king and in the state. The festering corruption of the garden springs directly from the 'disorder'd spring' (III. iv. 48) of Richard's own self-enclosure, his withdrawal from public concerns to the private, Narcissistic world of idleness and flattery. The garden is a supremely appropriate image through which to make the link between individual solitude and social disorder, since its associations with both enclosure and the commonwealth were traditional.[13] The image communicates simultaneously the self-consuming nature of Richard's isolation in his own inner world and its destructive effect on his kingdom.

Responsibility for a kingdom divided against itself is not entirely Richard's, however; Bolingbroke is the one who inherits the anti-social quality of dissembling from Richard III and who incites rebellion against the king. It is to him that Carlisle's warning, so reminiscent of the prophecies in *Richard III* and in so much other contemporary literature berating the times, is addressed:

> tumultuous wars
> Shall kin with kin and kind with kind confound;
> Disorder, horror, fear, and mutiny,
> Shall here inhabit, and this land be call'd
> The field of Golgotha and dead men's skulls.
> O, if you raise this house against this house,
> It will the woefullest division prove
> That ever fell upon this cursed earth.
>
> (IV. i. 140–7)

It is Bolingbroke and his son who continue the progress of division and fragmentation within the self through the rest of this history tetralogy. In a sense the progress from *Richard II* to *Henry V* is a progress from singleness of being to multiplicity. Philip Edwards, who distinguishes these two types of being as the continuum between person and office and the plastic self which adapts itself to any role, wonders 'how far . . . these two views of man represent

Shakespeare's recognition of an historical change in the nature of the relation between the individual and society'.[14] I have argued in Part One of this book that there was such a change, manifested in a growing preference for solitude over society, for inward over outward truth, for individual will over societal expectation. Such a valuing of the subjective and personal over the objective and communal is accompanied by an increased sense of the relativism of any truth, and by the fragmentation of old absolutes into multiple perspectives. The individual can no longer be depicted as a type, playing a stable part in a whole composed of stable moral absolutes; he becomes instead the sum of his own experiences, the creature of the moment. Instead of being fixed and defined by his place in the world, the world becomes fluid and indefinite under the lens of his mind. Montaigne is the most direct exponent of the fluidity and fragmentariness invading conceptions of both the self and its environment in the sixteenth century. One of his most famous passages formulates it in personal terms:

> I describe not the essence, but the passage . . . My history must be fitted to the present, I may soone change, not onely fortune, but intention. It is a counter-roule of divers and variable accidents, and irresolute imaginations, and sometimes contrary: whether it be that my selfe am other, or that I apprehend subjects, by other circumstances and considerations. Howsoever, I may perhaps gaine-say my selfe, but truth (as Demades said) I never gaine-say: Were my mind setled, I would not essay, but resolve my selfe.[15]

The progress from *Richard II* to *Henry IV* and *Henry V* is from the resistance to the acceptance of this view. Richard is shown to be fragmented, inconstant, given to adopting different roles, but unable to accept these qualities in himself. He seems to feel that static, absolute qualities are inherently better than fluid, relative ones, and tries to freeze each of his poses as he adopts it, to become the static emblem of his feelings. His images are most characteristically tableaux, and the ceremonial quality of both his language and his actions exhibits his need to see himself as an icon, to think of his being as fixed and to prolong each moment as it threatens to change. Henry IV and Henry V, by contrast, cultivate this ability to fragment themselves, keeping their inward selves uncommunicated and manipulating their public roles to best advantage. They cultivate the remoteness which keeps those around them guessing, uncertain of their true natures, Henry IV by keeping public appearances to a minimum and never revealing his emotions (except briefly to his son) and Prince Hal by withholding any emotional commitment from what his father labels his 'vile participation' (*1H4*, III. ii. 87). Falstaff recognises the real aloofness behind the facade of social engagement and tells him, in apparent jest: 'There's neither honesty, manhood, nor good fellowship in thee' (*1H4*, I. ii. 134–5).

The medieval world, where, in the Elizabethan imagination at least, men valued the bonds of kinship and society more highly than any individual preferences and made the common good their first priority, is fading in *Richard II*. The older men in the play, like York and John of Gaunt, try to restrain the anti-social impulses of Richard and Bolingbroke by reminding them of their natural bonds, whether as cousin to cousin, subject to king, or king to subjects and state. But the structure of the play emphasises the superseding of these social values by self-centred ones. Gaunt dies early in the play, York transfers his allegiance from Richard to Bolingbroke when the latter becomes king, and Richard and Bolingbroke themselves move towards increasingly intense isolation. The prison of Richard's solipsism becomes physical as well as spiritual in Act V, and in the complex of his thoughts the prison comes to stand for the body and the mind as well as the four walls around him.[16] Ironically, he first sees his physical solitude in prison as a barrier to a comparison between the prison and the world:

> I have been studying how I may compare
> This prison where I live unto the world;
> And, for because the world is populous
> And here is not a creature but myself,
> I cannot do it.   (v. v. 1–5)

Gradually he reaches towards the perception that the audience has had throughout, that he himself is his whole world, within or without the prison:

> Yet I'll hammer it out.
> My brain I'll prove the female to my soul,
> My soul the father; and these two beget
> A generation of still-breeding thoughts,
> And these same thoughts people this little world,
> In humours like the people of this world,
> For no thought is contented.   (5–11)

His inner isolation is embodied in this image of physical solitude just before his death, so that the implication that his solitariness has been literally self-consuming is unavoidable. His progress has been towards increasingly claustrophobic isolation within the inner world, and when this isolation reaches an absolute, combining his inner enclosure with physical solitary confinement, his death is inevitable. As in *Richard III*, Shakespeare, despite his increased sympathy for the solitude of Richard II, shows his disengagement from social concerns and devotion to the self leading inexorably towards death.

The play ends, however, not with the widening of the focus to concentrate on the reintegrating society, as in *Richard III*, but with the intensification of Henry IV's isolation, seeming to suggest Shakespeare's recognition of solitariness as a widespread, even inevitable, condition, not the state of the exceptional individual, or 'villain'. Henry's development inversely parallels Richard's: whereas Richard's inner solitude finds its physical counterpart at the end of the play, Henry's early physical exile finds its most intense inner counterpart in his guilt for Richard's murder. He himself makes a reference to the solitude of Cain in imposing the sentence of exile on Exton, who performed the murder:

> The guilt of conscience take thou for thy labour,
> But neither my good word nor princely favour;
> With Cain go wander thorough shades of night,
> And never show thy head by day nor light,
>
> (v. vi. 41-4)

but the pronouncement applies more directly to himself, since the moral responsibility for Richard's death rests with him. He is the real Cain, and the last words of the play do not move outwards from himself to his plans for society, but anticipate the intensification of his self-imprisonment through guilt and grief:

> I'll make a voyage to the Holy Land,
> To wash this blood off from my guilty hand.
> March sadly after; grace my mournings here
> In weeping after this untimely bier.   (49-52)

His inability to reach the Holy Land throughout the next two plays is the image of his inability to escape from the isolation which closes round him here, at the end of *Richard II*.

6 'Walls of glass':
The Sonnets

One of the most striking characteristics of the Sonnets is their obsessive repetition of the word 'self', which occurs more frequently here than in any other one of Shakespeare's works. It was not until the sixteenth century that 'self' came to be used as an autonomous noun; before then it occurred only as an element of reflexive pronouns. The progress of the word towards autonomy was part of a progress towards increasing autonomy in the actual concept of the self, which was coming to be defined more and more with reference to its own inner world, rather than through its external contexts. The beginnings of autonomy can be seen in the repetition of the reflexive in Petrarch's sonnets and Montaigne's essays, although the equivalents of 'self' in their languages did not actually attain grammatical autonomy. Shakespeare's Sonnets, on the other hand, show quite clearly the breaking down of the boundaries between reflexive and autonomous usage from the very first sonnet:

Thyself thy foe, to thy sweet self too cruel   (Son. 1)

Thou of thyself thy sweet self dost deceive   (Son. 4)

To give away your self keeps your self still   (Son. 16)

Variations among modern editors in printing 'thyself' or 'thyself' confirm the fluidity of the boundaries.

Almost as characteristic as the repetition of 'self' standing alone or in a pronoun is the prevalence of compound words with 'self': 'self-substantial' (Son. 1), 'self-love' (Son. 3), 'self-kill'd (Son. 6), 'self-will'd' (Son. 6). The inevitable implications of self-division attaching to such words demonstrate the way the preoccupation with the self in this period was linked almost by definition with a sense of inward division.

From even the small number of lines quoted so far from the Sonnets it is evident that the first sonnet, and by extension the first group of six sonnets, like Richard iii's first soliloquy, sets out most of the themes and images of the sequence as a whole.[1] Many of those themes and images are the same as those outlined in Richard's soliloquy. Even the linguistic emblem of the self isolated within its own circularity, Richard's 'myself myself', is transformed in the Sonnets into the patterns of 'thyself thyself' and 'yourself yourself' (see quotations above), and linked with echoes of 'I am myself alone':

> For having traffic with thyself alone,
> Thou of thyself thy sweet self dost deceive.   (Son. 4)

The 'thyself alone' and 'thyself thyself' patterns are condemnatory in this instance, where they are followed by an exhortation to exchange this sterile self-enclosure for the satisfaction of breeding other selves:

> That's for thyself to breed an other thee,
> Or ten times happier, be it ten for one;
> Ten times thy self were happier than thou art,
> If ten of thine ten times refigur'd thee.   (Son. 6)

Giorgio Melchiori has noted how frequently the second person occurs in Shakespeare's Sonnets, by contrast with other contemporary sonnet sequences, interpreting this to be an indication that Shakespeare's love takes the form of a real dialogue between equals, rather than a distant reverence. 'The characteristic feature of Shakespeare's Sonnets', he writes, 'as compared with those of his contemporaries is the balanced predominance of *I* and *thou* rather than the distance between *I* and *she*.'[2] This is true in one sense and distorting in another, for the use of the second person often seems to convey the very distance between the poet and his cold love, particularly when it occurs as part of this pattern of self-loving disengagement on the part of the boy, 'thyself thyself'.

The constant urging of the boy towards marriage, fertility and reproduction in the early sonnets embodies an attempt to dissuade him from the metaphorically sterile life of detachment and self-interest as well as from actual sterility. Other aspects of the language besides this 'thyself thyself' pattern mimic sterility. The reflexive verb *per se*, without repetition, is a potentially 'self-consuming' element, and Shakespeare repeatedly uses it in the Sonnets to show how actions performed within the circle of the self instead of beyond it become thwarted and self-negating. The reversal of an outward action by forcing it inward is self-destructive:

> thou consum'st thyself in single life . . .
> beauty's waste hath in the world an end,
> And kept unus'd, the user so destroys it.   (Son. 9)

> Grant, if thou wilt, thou art belov'd of many,
> But that thou none lov'st is most evident;
> For thou art so possess'd with murd'rous hate
> That gainst thyself thou stick'st not to conspire,
> Seeking that beauteous roof to ruinate
> Which to repair should be thy chief desire.   (Son. 10)

>   to you it doth belong
> Your self to pardon of self-doing crime.   (Son. 58)

The only action which could reverse itself to the boy's advantage is the one which would take him outside himself:

> To give away your self keeps your self still. (Son. 16)

Reciprocity, the reverse of the boy's closed inwardness, is the only source of true fulfilment:

> Then happy I, that love and am beloved
> Where I may not remove nor be removed.   (Son. 25)

From the first sonnet, the equation between spiritual self-consumption and physical death is explicit:

> Thou that art now the world's fresh ornament
> And only herald to the gaudy spring,
> Within thine own bud buriest thy content,
> And, tender churl, mak'st waste in niggarding.
> Pity the world, or else this glutton be,
> To eat the world's due, by the grave and thee,

anticipating the bitter invective against this same inner rotting in
Sonnet 94:

> Lilies that fester smell far worse than weeds.

The flower imagery in both instances is reminiscent of the Narcissus
myth. Bacon's condemnation of the solitary, inward tendencies of
the Narcissus-type has been quoted in part above (p. 29), but the
end of his commentary is more directly relevant to the Sonnets in its
association of the flower Narcissus with futility and death. Bacon,
referring to the disappointment of early promise in maturity, writes:

> The fact too that this flower is sacred to the infernal deities
> contains an allusion to the same thing. For men of this disposition
> turn out utterly useless and good for nothing whatever; and
> anything that yields no fruit, but like the way of a ship in the sea
> passes and leaves no trace, was by the ancients held sacred to the
> shades and infernal gods.[3]

The image of the glass in the Sonnets, as in *Richard III* and *Richard
II*, supports the interpretation of the young man as a Narcissus type,
Sonnet 3, for example, plays on the double potential of the reflected
image to be seen as either the propagation or the imprisonment of
the self:

> Look in thy glass, and tell the face thou viewest
> Now is the time that face should form another . . .
> Thou art thy mother's glass, and she in thee
> Calls back the lovely April of her prime;
> So thou through windows of thine age shalt see,
> Despite of wrinkles, this thy golden time.
> But if thou live rememb'red not to be,
> Die single, and thine image dies with thee.

As for Richard II, glass can be looked through as a means of
transcending the limits of self, or into, imprisoning the self within
those same limits. It can suggest the sense of liberation from the
confines of the self, or the claustrophobia within them.[4] The images
of glass as mirror and window are extended into the glass vial of
Sonnets 5 and 6. The vial, though ostensibly the image of the
propagation of self, the 'distillation' of the self's image in the next

generation, actually suggests, against the syntactical sense, the closed world of the single boy. The line

A liquid prisoner pent in walls of glass, (Son. 5)

despite its actual reference to the distilled flower which represents the boy's imagined child, ironically suggests more strongly the imprisonment of the single, uncommitted boy, who is enclosed in a world of mirrors.

The terminology of shadows too, associated with the mirror in *Richard II* and *Richard III*,[5] implies the weakness, insubstantiality and delusion of the self-lover. The young man is 'a weakened being whose activity is crippled',[6] a figure stunted inwardly, by contrast with his physical beauty (unlike Richard III, whose inner deformity is given an external image). As in these two plays, Shakespeare does not allow the individual to be defined wholly from within in the way to which he aspires, but measures him against the framework he rejects, a framework which will finally overwhelm him in the shape of time and death. From first to last, the Sonnets warn that the individual's rejection of the world outside him cannot be an absolute. However hard an individual may try to erect himself into his absolute, and define the world as relative only to his inner self, his subjective truth, his mortality will in fact prove that it is he who is the mere relative, and the enclosing framework of the world the absolute. Only a creative act on the part of the individual, an act which moves beyond the self to recognise society, whether it be producing a child or writing poetry, can confer immortality on the individual and enable him to overcome time and death. He transcends the constants of the framework by becoming part of it, not by denying its existence.

The boy's position in relation to society can be summed up by the word 'singleness', to which Shakespeare attributes a widely suggestive semantic range. Most obviously, the word describes the boy's marital status. Being single, he will die without a child, and therefore remain self-contained, single also in that sense:

Die single, and thine image dies with thee. (Son. 3)

He is single in the sense that he is a part cut off from the whole, a solitary individual without a social context. The vocabulary of 'concord' and 'union' which Shakespeare applies to marriage also suggests the greater social order of which the family was a recognised image:[7]

> If the true concord of well-tuned sounds,
> By unions married, do offend thine ear,
> They do but sweetly chide thee, who confounds
> In singleness the parts that thou shouldst bear.   (Son. 8)

'Singleness' suggests too his proud aloofness from other men, the way he holds himself apart from commitment to others, and the preciousness implied by that aloofness. Sonnet 94, despite its bitter denunciation of the rottenness likely to destroy such a one, demonstrates simultaneously an admiration for such self-sufficiency and invulnerability:

> They that have power to hurt and will do none,
> That do not do the thing they most do show,
> Who, moving others, are themselves as stone,
> Unmoved, cold, and to temptation slow—
> They rightly do inherit Heaven's graces,
> And husband nature's riches from expense;
> They are the lords and owners of their faces,
> Others but stewards of their excellence.

Even the flower image, besides evoking the self-consumption of Narcissus, also suggests the fragile and delicate beauty of solipsistic singleness:

> The summer's flow'r is to the summer sweet
> Though to itself it only live and die.

The quality of singleness, or 'singularity', suggests two kinds of isolation: the voluntary detachment and self-containment described in 'Unmoved, cold, and to temptation slow' and the inherent distinctiveness or superiority implied by the inheritance of 'Heaven's graces'. The boy is singled out from other men not only by his wilful affectation and self-love, but by the distinctive quality which makes him what he is, his 'singularity'. And this singularity, of course, his lover cannot condemn, but can only praise (in another echo of Richard III's phrase):

> Who is it that says most which can say more
> Than this rich praise—that you alone are you?   (Son. 84)

Yet this exalts that aspect of nature which distinguishes men and makes them individuals at the expense of the nature which unites them in that they are all men. The boy does not recognise nature in the general sense, the nature that makes him a man like other men, but recognises only his own particular nature, the nature that singles him out from other men. Praise of this second kind of nature was becoming common in the sixteenth century, as individual autonomy was gaining wider recognition. Ralegh, for example, praises the nature that separates and distinguishes rather than the nature which unites and identifies:

> But such is the multiplying and extensive vertue of dead Earth, and of that breath-giving life which GOD hath cast upon Slime and Dust: as that . . . every one hath received a severall picture of face, and everie one a diverse picture of minde; every one a forme apart, every one a fancy and cogitation differing, there being nothing wherein Nature so much triumpheth, as in dissimilitude.[8]

And just as the emphasis on individual nature characteristically accompanies an emphasis on the inward self, just as the boy of the Sonnets chooses his own inner world in preference to the outside world, so Ralegh emphasises that distinction and definition are located within, in the mind, not in the external public self or its context: ' . . . it is not the visible fashion and shape of plants, and of reasonable Creatures, that makes the difference, of working in the one, and of condition in the other; but the forme internall.'[9]

The most conspicuous point about Shakespeare's reference to the boy as 'single', however, is the irony inherent in the use of such a word to describe one who is fickle and inwardly fragmented. Living entirely within the circle of self, he is in one sense single in his isolation, but in another divided, in that he himself must play the role of both agent and object, must be both active and passive in all his purely self-referential actions. He is divided too on a more superficial level, in exhibiting, like Richard III, a division between face and heart: where Richard's innocent face hides his guilt, the young man's beautiful face hides his treacherous, faithless soul.

Even his sexuality bears the marks of division, in that he is physically a man, but has the beauty of a woman and accepts a man as lover. Above all, he is changeable, living, like Richard II, only for the moment, betraying the self he seems or the role he plays from sonnet to sonnet. He is unfaithful to the poet in his acceptance of the dark lady as a lover and in his dallying with the favours of the rival poet; he is unreliable and unstable in his response to the poet even without outside influences:

> Thy self thou gav'st, thy own worth then not knowing,
> Or me, to whom thou gav'st it, else mistaking;
> So thy great gift, upon misprision growing,
> Comes home again, on better judgment making.   (Son. 87)

As in *Richard II*, however, where the presentation of Richard's solitude is qualified by comparison with solitude from Bolingbroke's perspective, so the withdrawal and self-division of the boy in the Sonnets do not constitute a single, unchallenged judgement of these qualities. The poet comes progressively to feel the existence in himself of those qualities he has condemned in the boy. In the early poems of the sequence he presents himself as wholly opposed to the boy's detachment and rejection of commitment. He speaks with the voice of society in urging the boy to take a wife and beget a child, thus embracing the values and social bonds of the world to which he belongs. But gradually, as the poet becomes more and more absorbed by the boy who tantalises him, he finds himself increasingly alienated from society, increasingly contained by his own inner world, subjective in his values and judgements, and remote from public concerns. The first person, not even introduced until the tenth sonnet, becomes more prominent and more isolated. Sonnet 29 describes the passing sense of desolation:

> When in disgrace with Fortune and men's eyes,
> I all alone beweep my outcast state,
> And trouble deaf heaven with my bootless cries,
> And look upon myself, and curse my fate,

for which he finds comfort in love by retreating from it into a private world. Sonnet 79 recalls fondly the time when he stood alone in the boy's love, glorying in this singularity:

Whilst I alone did call upon thy aid,
My verse alone had all thy gentle grace.

Sonnet 131 echoes Richard III's familiar phrase, the expression of
one who sets his own values against those of society, in a context
which seems to justify autonomy:

some say that thee behold
Thy face hath not the power to make love groan.
To say they err I dare not be so bold,
Although I swear it to myself alone.

Richard's 'I am I' is also echoed, in a more defiant tone of
justification, in Sonnet 121: 'No; I am that I am.' The fact that the
poet himself utters the challenge of self-definition, and not the boy,
or any character clearly worthy of condemnation, suggests that
Shakespeare's response to self-definition is no longer simply one of
moral condemnation, and that the feeling of admiring awe which
seemed sporadically present in *Richard III* is becoming more
dominant than the sense of moral outrage. In this context it brings
to mind not only Jehovah's 'I AM', but also St Paul's legitimate,
because qualified, self-definition: '. . . by the grace of God, I am
that I am' (1 Cor. 15:10; see p. 29 above). St Paul's statement is
compatible with Pico's well-known exaltation of man's capacity for
self-definition. God, according to Pico, having made man,

. . . & doubting with what maner of life he shuld adorne this his
newe heire, this divine artificer, in the ende determined to make
him unto whom hee could not assigne any thing in proper,
partaker of al that, which the others enjoyed but in particular,
whereupon calling him unto him, he sayd: Live O *Adam*, in what
life pleaseth thee best, and take unto thy self those gifts which
thou esteemest most deare. From this so liberall a graunt . . . had
our free wil his original, so that it is in our power, to live like a
plant, living creature, like a man, & lastly as an Angell: for if a
man addict himself only to feeding and nourishment, hee
becommeth a Plante, if to things sensuall, he is as a brute beast, if
to things reasonable & civil, he groweth a celestial creature: but if
he exalt the beautiful gift of his mind, to thinges invisible and
divine, hee transfourmeth himselfe into an Angel; and to
conclude, becommeth the sonne of God.[10]

The Sonnets share with Pico the conception of the individual as fluid, self-defining and preoccupied with the inner world in place of externals. The 'I am that I am' that could be condemned as heresy and a rejection of moral values in Richard III has become transformed into the more morally ambiguous and sympathetic quality of truth to self.

Melchiori considers that the echoing of God's 'I AM' in this phrase in Sonnet 121 implies that 'Shakespeare's God is the man within'.[11] But the increasing emphasis on inwardness in the Sonnets is surely not so unequivocally exalted. As the poet becomes more isolated from the external world he can no longer simply condemn such inner enclosure as he might have done if it had been characteristic only of the boy, but in recognising an increasing inwardness in himself his reaction is not changed to unqualified admiration, since he also feels the torment of his imprisonment. As he becomes more completely identified with his inward self and the love that dominates it, so he can no longer clearly distinguish between himself and the boy, no longer withdraw to judge the boy from the world's perspective. It is the external world from which he has withdrawn to the point where the inner world has become his whole world:

> As easy might I from my self depart
> As from my soul, which in thy breast doth lie . . .
> For nothing this wide universe I call
> Save thou, my rose; in it thou art my all   (Son. 109)

> You are my all the world . . .
> You are so strongly in my purpose bred
> That all the world besides methinks are dead.   (Son. 112)

As for Richard II, the world has become for him a totally subjective experience, a mirror-image of the inner self. Each external impression reflects the perceiving self more clearly than its own essence, as the poet confesses:

> Since I left you, mine eye is in my mind;
> And that which governs me to go about
> Doth part his function, and is partly blind,
> Seems seeing, but effectually is out;
> For it no form delivers to the heart

Of bird, of flow'r, or shape, which it doth latch . . .
For if it see the rud'st or gentlest sight . . .
           it shapes them to your feature.
Incapable of more, replete with you,
My most true mind thus mak'th mine eye untrue.
                          (Son. 113)

Like the boy, though involuntarily, the poet is becoming increasingly bound in to the prison of the inward self.

The mirror, image of the restrictiveness of such disproportionate subjectivity, becomes important to the poet as well as to the vain boy:

My glass shall not persuade me I am old
So long as youth and thou are of one date;   (Son. 22)

Sin of self-love possesseth all mine eye,
And all my soul, and all my every part . . .
But when my glass shows me myself indeed,
Beated and chopt with tann'd antiquity,
Mine own self-love quite contrary I read;
Self so self-loving were iniquity.
'Tis thee, my self, that for myself I praise,
Painting my age with beauty of thy days.   (Son. 62)

It is clear that there is a difference in the way the boy and the poet look into their glasses. The boy sees only his own image; the poet sees his own image inextricably bound up with that of the boy, to whom his commitment is total. The boy is so much part of him that he thinks of him as a second self, and this conceit dominates the Sonnets so that self-love and love, in the poet at least, become indistinguishable.

This transformation of self-love into love of another, however, is not really an escape from the solipsistic circle framed by the mirror. The notion of the lover as second self may imply that self-love is transformed into outgoing love; or it may imply the opposite, that all love is really a form of self-love. A peculiarly Elizabethan image, the image of 'looking babies', whereby one lover looks in the other's eyes only to see his or her own reflection in them, is a variation on the image of the glass which makes this ironical observation unmistakable.[12] The irony that love, which would seem to be a way

of breaking out of the circle of self-absorption, is in fact another way
of reinforcing that circle, is heavily underlined in *Venus and Adonis*.
Adonis, like the boy of the Sonnets, seems to be the Narcissist,
refusing all love and entirely absorbed in his own image, but it is
Venus who sees her own image in Adonis's eyes. Venus speaks an
elegy over Adonis's dead body, but can describe his beauty only in
terms of its capacity to reflect her. His eyes seem to her to be

> Two glasses where herself herself beheld
> A thousand times, and now no more reflect,
> Their virtue lost wherein they late excell'd,
> And every beauty robb'd of his effect.   (ll. 1129–32)

The characteristic 'herself herself' pattern seems to confirm the
implication of the 'looking babies' image, that Venus's love for
Adonis was in fact as self-absorbed as Adonis's more obvious self-
love.

The repeated image of the lover as a second self in the Sonnets
performs the same function as the 'looking babies' image, suggesting
the poet's doubt about the quality of his own love, his fear that it
may be in fact as narcissistic as the boy's frank self-love. He tries to
qualify the image of the second self in order to maintain the
necessary distinctness between himself and his lover which enables
their love to be thought of as a reciprocal rather than a solipsistic
experience, and which prevents praise from becoming self-
congratulation:

> O, how thy worth with manners may I sing,
> When thou art all the better part of me?
> What can mine own praise to mine own self bring?
> And what is't but mine own, when I praise thee?
> Even for this let us divided live,
> And our dear love lose name of single one,
> That by this separation I may give
> That due to thee which thou deserv'st alone.   (Son. 39)

He wants to keep his love set apart as a unique being, distanced from
his own sense of unworthiness:

> Let me confess that we two must be twain,
> Although our undivided loves are one;

> So shall those blots that do with me remain,
> Without thy help, by me be borne alone.   (Son. 36)

Even the contradictoriness of the poet's feelings, however, his uncertainty as to whether he longs for fusion with or separateness from his love, shows him becoming like the boy in another way, by exhibiting a form of self-division. Just as the boy betrays the image he last presented from moment to moment, so the poet finds himself responding to this fickleness in the boy with a comparable instability. He even offers literally to turn against himself and to frustrate his own actions voluntarily (as the boy's self-love involuntarily frustrates his):

> When thou shalt be dispos'd to set me light,
> And place my merit in the eye of scorn,
> Upon thy side against myself I'll fight,
> And prove thee virtuous, though thou art forsworn
> (Son. 88)

> For thee, against myself I'll vow debate,
> For I must ne'er love him whom thou dost hate.   (Son. 89)

Such inward division comes to resemble the boy's even more strongly when the dark lady enters the sequence and the poet is no longer faithful to one love, but divided between two in his affections.

The self-division of the lover is not, of course, an innovation of Shakespeare's, but familiar in Petrarch and the tradition inspired by him. Yet Shakespeare's emphasis seems to imply that the self-division he explores is perhaps in the nature of self-awareness rather than simply induced by love. The sheer repetition of the word 'self' suggests that his Sonnets are more concerned with the nature of the self than with love *per se*. Sonnet 144, for example, shows the poet divided between his two loves, but the division originating in love is used as a mere starting point to explore a more deeply-rooted division within all men, a division given expression in morality plays by the good and evil angels who accompany every man:

> Two loves I have, of comfort and despair,
> Which like two spirits do suggest me still;
> The better angel is a man right fair,
> The worser spirit a woman colour'd ill.

Besides its medieval origins, this division of man between his capacities to be either angel or devil is directly reminiscent of the passage from Pico's *Oration on the Dignity of Man* quoted on p. 85 above, which admires the unique fluidity of man's position in the universe. This passage measures the distance between the classical and the Renaissance conceptions of man: whereas Aristotle conceives of man as occupying a fixed place in the universal hierarchy, and becoming inhuman in behaving like a god or a beast, thus taking a strongly moral stance concerning human action, Pico sees the capacity for self-definition, for autonomous self-creation, as the distinguishing feature of man.

The Sonnets too are characteristic of late sixteenth-century England by virtue of their recognition of this autonomy which the self achieves through becoming aware of its own inward nature and the immense transforming power of subjectivity. The closed inwardness and self-contained quality of each sonnet, the refusal of one sonnet to be bound by the self-images offered by other sonnets, the fluidity of the sequence, in which each sonnet seems to embody a truth which holds true only for the moment in which it is stated, are poetic characteristics which imitate these same qualities within the self. The sonnet, like the individual, asserts its own autonomy in this period, by resolving the paradoxes of experience in the terms of its own self-created world. Like Richard II, the speaker in the Sonnets substitutes the private world for the public, or forces the public world into subservience to the private, so that words themselves come to have a paradoxical relationship with the speaker and his world, in that they both communicate the private experience, yet at the same time isolate the speaker within the subjective nature of that experience. The autonomy of the individual is revealed in his transformation of actual experience through words; where the experience itself is unsatisfactory or unresolved, the poet finds a resolution in the linguistic but arbitrary logic of a conceit:

> But here's the joy: my friend and I are one;
> Sweet flattery! then she loves but me alone.   (Son. 42)

> Look what is best, that best I wish in thee;
> This wish I have; then ten times happy me!   (Son. 37)

> And all in war with Time for love of you,
> As he takes from you, I engraft you new.   (Son. 15)

So shalt thou feed on Death, that feeds on men,
And, Death once dead, there's no more dying then.
(Son. 146)

The Sonnets show the world of the mind dominating the individual vision of the external world and demonstrating its power over the material world by imposing its own pattern on the experiences it does not resolve to the individual's satisfaction. The sonnet is a perfect form, as the mirror is a perfect image, for expressing the withdrawal of the individual into the inescapable and autonomous solitude of the mind.

7 'For other than for dancing measures': *As You Like It*

Renaissance pastoral clearly focuses the division characteristic of the period. Like the prose debates on solitude, it attempts to reconcile opposites or modify them to a point of similarity, but offers, instead of argument, an aesthetic resolution of the tension between sociability and solitude, between the active and contemplative lives. Pastoral portrays a way of life associated with the contemplative ideal, with retirement, privacy, reflectiveness and simplicity; but it presents this contemplative ideal in a social context, showing a microcosmic society, instead of an individual, retiring from public life to the woods. In this way the absolutes of contemplative solitude and active civil life are qualified to the point where they meet in the middle, in the ethos of an introspective society, withdrawn from the world of business, free both to enjoy the pleasures of company and to substitute meditation and self-examination for the burdens of public life. Sidney describes the ability of pastoral to lessen the distance between extremes in a very literal way when he writes that the houses in Arcadia are 'all scattered, no two being one by th'other, & yet not so far off as that it barred mutual succour: a shew, as it were, of an accompanable solitarines & of a civil wildnes'.[1] Oxymorons emphasise the convergence of opposites.

Both pastoral and its theoretical counterpart, the treatise praising the life of the country and dispraising that of the court, have classical origins, and only their prevalence at this time, not their originality as forms, indicates their particular association with the sixteenth and early seventeenth centuries. The preoccupation with pastoral ideas at this time is confirmed in retrospect too by the important semantic developments taking place in such words as 'country', 'rural', 'rustic', 'farm' and 'pastoral' itself.[2]

Renato Poggioli has distinguished three forms of pastoral: the pastoral of innocence, which is based on the community; the pastoral of happiness, based on the couple; and the pastoral of the self, based on the individual seen in solitude.[3] He devotes an essay to the subject of this last form of pastoral, finding it to be one of the latest developments in its history:

> Contrary to one's expectations, bucolic poetry was not predestined to sing the praises of solitude. It was only toward the end of its long historical life that the pastoral ever fulfilled what may well be the most congenial of its many tasks. The theme of solitude is almost totally absent from Theocritus' *Idylls* and Vergil's *Eclogues*, and it is never central in the pastorals of the Renaissance. Its appearances before the seventeenth century are fleeting; the role that solitude plays up to then on the pastoral stage is only that of an extra or, at the most, of a minor character.[4]

Shakespeare's *As You Like It* plays a major part in the development of pastoral towards this solitary mode, by allowing Jaques to become so important a figure in the scheme. It carefully balances the claims of solitude (here equated with melancholy) against those of love and union with another (equated with happiness) through the opposition between Jaques and the rest of society, particularly Orlando. Poggioli quotes their parting, in which they clearly label one another:

> *Jaq.* I'll tarry no longer with you; farewell, good Signior Love.
> *Oral.* I am glad of your departure; adieu, good Monsieur
> Melancholy. (III. ii. 274–7)

as an obvious statement of this antithesis.[5] Jaques and the pastoral of solitude which he embodies are Shakespeare's own addition to his source, his own innovation in a received tradition. The self-analytical nature of Jaques and of the play as a whole clearly anticipates the seventeenth-century pastoral of the self in solitude, 'where the retreat into Arcadia is in reality a retreat into the soul, with no company except the self'.[6]

As You Like It is a highly self-conscious, inward-looking play, displaying its awareness of its own style, conventions, sources and the contemporary world in which its performance takes place. When Orlando enters one scene with the words:

Good day, and happiness, dear Rosalind!   (IV. i. 27)

Jaques takes his leave with this observation:

Nay, then, God buy you, an you talk in blank verse.
(28–9)

Even the literary criticism surrounding pastoral and art generally is openly referred to in the phrase 'golden world'[7] which Charles the wrestler adopts in describing Duke Senior's retreat to the forest:

They say he is already in the Forest of Arden, and a many merry men with him; and there they live like the old Robin Hood of England. They say many young gentlemen flock to him every day, and fleet the time carelessly, as they did in the golden world. (I. i. 105–9)

The reference to Robin Hood also draws attention to the immediate medieval past of Renaissance England, to which it looks back more realistically than to the idealised golden age of the classics. Nevertheless, the idea of medieval England presented in *As You Like It*, though more topical than the classical golden age, is still somewhat idealised. It is made clear at the beginning of the play that the values most revered are those of the past, as represented in old Adam, who upholds the social duties of service and loyalty. Orlando speaks a formal eulogy of the past in acknowledging Adam's loyalty to him:

O good old man, how well in thee appears
The constant service of the antique world,
When service sweat for duty, not for meed!
Thou art not for the fashion of these times,
Where none will sweat but for promotion,
And having that do choke their service up
Even with the having; it is not so with thee.
(II. iii. 56–62)

The deterioration of relationships and the rise of self-interest in Orlando's times as compared with Adam's are demonstrated in Oliver's treatment of Orlando, which Adam describes in terms that evoke the familiar homilies of Shakespeare's own times (see pp. 29, 57 and 73 above):

> Your brother—no, no brother; yet the son—
> Yet not the son; I will not call him son
> Of him I was about to call his father—
> Hath heard your praises; and this night he means
> To burn the lodging where you use to lie,
> And you within it. If he fail of that,
> He will have other means to cut you off;
> I overheard him and his practices.
> This is no place; this house is but a butchery;
> Abhor it, fear it, do not enter it.   (II. iii. 19–28)

The medieval ideal is clearly invoked too by the appearance of a religious hermit and by the emphasis on the attractions of the contemplative life throughout the play. This is the only one of Shakespeare's plays which ends with the decisions of two characters, Jaques and Duke Frederick, to withdraw from the life of mutual participation to which the others are returning, in favour of a life of solitary contemplation. In one sense the play thus returns very much to reality at its close, not only in the Epilogue's metamorphosis of Rosalind into the boy-actor who plays her, but also in the rejection of the artificial solution of pastoral. Shakespeare, in turning away from the artificial reconciliation of the two lives contained in pastoral, and showing them splitting apart again at the end into irreconcilable absolutes, recognises the reality of the conflict between the solitary and the social lives which preoccupied his times, and demonstrates the sophistry of art's solutions.

Of these two who choose the solitary extreme at the end, only Duke Frederick does so in the true medieval spirit, offering penitence and devotion in reparation for his evil worldly life. Jaques chooses a much more sixteenth-century solitude, choosing in a spirit of sceptical enquiry and experiment.[8] He remains an observer, refusing to commit himself, thus placing himself in direct opposition to the total commitment demanded by the medieval religious ideal. Whereas Duke Frederick is actually 'converted . . . from the world' (v. iv. 155–6), Jaques only wants to question the converted:

> To him will I. Out of these convertites
> There is much matter to be heard and learn'd.
>
>   (v. iv. 178–9)

Jaques stands out by virtue of his non-commitment, since both the other choices, Duke Frederick's choice of religious contemplation and the others' choice of social harmony, are medieval in their recognition of an order beyond the individual, and their commitment to such an order. The movement of the group back to the bonds of family life and social responsibility, to a world where church and commonwealth are one and men are united in fellowship and mutual compassion (see e.g. II. vii. 120–3) is as much an expression of nostalgia as the movement of those individuals who are 'for other than for dancing measures' (v. iv. 187) towards the inner order of the contemplative life. Perhaps the co-existence of both at the end of the play is not so much the expression of a realism which refuses the reconcilements of art as of an idealism which looks back to a time when the solitary was the exception and society was stable enough to support the committed solitary contemplative without feeling his solitude to be an anti-social threat to the order of fellowship.

But there is still Jaques to account for, who does not really accept either of these alternatives, and his refusal to be reconciled is true to the spirit of irony and scepticism which pervades the rest of the play. Jaques threatens to undercut both alternatives offered at the end, both the social and the contemplative, by his refusal to participate in either. He questions these orderly solutions, and is a fragmenting and divisive influence on the ideals of love, marriage and good fellowship which bind society together. He is like an element imported out of another genre, and just as Richard III questioned the very dramatic conventions of the play in which he found himself, setting himself outside its structure, seeming more like the Vice of the morality play, or the machiavellian villain than a tragic hero, so Jaques is more like a satirist than a comic figure. Though the malcontent was a recognisable butt of ridicule in contemporary comedy, Jaques is more than ridiculous and his criticisms have to be taken seriously. In this respect he does resemble the satirist, whose typical qualities are outlined in this description by a modern critic, Alvin Kernan:

The satirist is above all harsh, honest, frank, and filled with indignation at the sight of the evil world where fools and villains prosper by masquerading as virtuous men . . . although he is the inveterate foe of vice, he himself has dark twists in his character: he is sadistic and enjoys his rough work; he is filled with envy of those same fools he despises and castigates; he has a taste for the sensational and delights in exposing those sins of which he is himself guilty; he is a sick man, his nature unbalanced by melancholy, whose perspective of the world is distorted by his malady.[9]

Pastoral can easily accommodate Jaques's criticism, both of the conventions of pastoral and of Shakespeare's own times beyond the world of the play. It is traditionally a highly self-conscious genre and as such well-suited to topical allusions and private jokes, for which it was notorious in the Renaissance. The pastoral life was the recognised image of a state of mind,[10] so the action is minimal and the characters very much given to meditation and self-examination. In this way pastoral can show, as it were, the mind of the community analysing and criticising itself, through the juxtaposition of different individual views. The play, like the pastoral life, behaves like a mind, demonstrating self-awareness and a capacity for introspection.

The self-analytical bent of *As You Like It* is shown in the first place by its proliferation of set speeches, which are pure meditation, as opposed to performing any expository function regarding action. Duke Senior's speech on the pastoral life is self-consciously traditional in its careful recapitulation of the familiar themes: comparison with the court, freedom from ambition and envy, a life in tune with nature, escape from flattery, the moral purity of the retired life. It is taken from a speech by Lodge's shepherd Coridon, which in turn draws on the lyrical tradition inspired by Virgil and Horace and on the treatises praising the country life. But the finely ironical self-appreciation of the play is shown by the various ways in which this conventional speech is undercut. Jaques's song, for example, is a crude deflation of pastoral high-mindedness, as exhibited by the Duke:

> If it do come to pass
> That any man turn ass,
> Leaving his wealth and ease
> A stubborn will to please,
> Ducdame, ducdame, ducdame;
> Here shall he see
> Gross fools as he,
> An if he will come to me.   (II. v. 46–53)

A far more virtuoso deflation is carried out by Touchstone in his speech on the pastoral life, which directly parodies the debates of the time by speaking both parts, and mimicking the qualifying, balancing, self-contradictory style. Only minimal exaggeration is necessary to make the whole debate look like specious nonsense:

> Truly, shepherd, in respect of itself, it is a good life; but in respect that it is a shepherd's life, it is nought. In respect that it is solitary, I like it very well; but in respect that it is private, it is a very vile life. Now in respect it is in the fields, it pleaseth me well; but in respect it is not in the court, it is tedious. As it is a spare life, look you, it fits my humour well; but as there is no more plenty in it, it goes much against my stomach. Hast any philosophy in thee, shepherd?[11] (III. ii. 13–21)

Like Jacques, Touchstone is an invention of Shakespeare's, not to be found in Lodge, and as such is particularly likely to offer detached observations which call into question the pastoral ethos. His very name is an indication of the way in which he acts as an evaluator of authenticity, unmasking poses and sophistry with his own peculiar pose and sophistry.

The undercutting of pastoral goes further. The shepherd has a reply to Touchstone's question which is steadfastly literal and down-to-earth, and makes an amusing comparison with his counterpart in Lodge, who speaks the idealised eulogy which Shakespeare gives the Duke. Corin restricts his philosophy to making remarks about the sheep and the weather, offering such penetrating illuminations of truth as 'that the property of rain is to wet, and fire to burn; that good pasture makes fat sheep; and that a great cause of the night is lack of the sun' (24–7). Despite his dull-wittedness, Corin exposes the pastoral life of the intruders as a mere courtly game, far removed from the necessities of a country life, and is perhaps Shakespeare's jibe at those courtiers in his own world who repeatedly expressed their longing for a retired, country life.

The co-existence of Silvius and Phebe and Audrey and William as inhabitants of the forest is another joke against the popular idealisation of the pastoral life. Silvius and Phebe are the literary types of pastoral, behaving like characters out of Lodge or any other straight romantic pastoral, but made to look ridiculous within the more sceptical framework of Shakespeare's play. They play their parts with the exaggerated attention to detail and deliberate conformity to type which characterises the adherents of a cult in the world outside the play. Silvius plays the Petrarchan lover whom Orlando refuses to play,[12] and shows how well he knows his part by formally listing the characteristics of the type he emulates, ending with the climactic affectation of solitude:

> Or if thou hast not broke from company
> Abruptly, as my passion now makes me,
> Thou hast not lov'd.
> O Phebe, Phebe, Phebe!   (II. iv. 37–40)

'Abruptly' exposes the self-consciousness of the affectation by letting Silvius betray his own absurdity in anticipating a supposedly uncontrollable impulse. Even before the laughter of the other characters, Silvius has unconsciously revealed the element of the ridiculous in his pose.

Phebe's letter to Rosalind (Ganymede) shows this same mixture of self-consciousness (in studying to follow the part of the cruel fair to the letter) and unself-consciousness (in failing to realise the absurdity of her pose in the eyes of others). Literary attitudinising is punctured by realism, as in the exchange between Touchstone and Corin, when Rosalind gives Phebe a realistic reason for demonstrating the conventional pity:

> Down on your knees,
> And thank heaven, fasting, for a good man's love;
> For I must tell you friendly in your ear:
> Sell when you can; you are not for all markets.
>   (III. v. 57–60)

Audrey and William reach beyond realism in the antithesis they present to the literary attitudinising of Silvius and Phebe. Their stupidity, coarseness and general 'foulness' is as exaggerated a conception of country people as the sophistication of Silvius and Phebe. Their co-existence with Silvius and Phebe is not Shakespeare's way of setting the reality against the literary idealisation, but rather his way of emphasising the subjectivity of point of view, and the relativism of reality. The title of the play, *As You Like It*, explicitly draws attention to the subjectivity of the individual response, and the play demonstrates this subjectivity throughout by the juxtaposition of characters, speeches and scenes.

Rosalind's advice to Phebe to recognise the very marked limitations of her own beauty is not necessarily any more objectively true than Phebe's opinion of herself, which is inspired in any case by Silvius's judgement. Before pronouncing her opinion, Rosalind draws attention to the subjectivity of the attitudes of Silvius and Phebe, thus necessarily placing her own opinion in such a context, whether or not she is aware of this logical extension of her remark:

> 'Tis not her glass, but you, that flatters her;
> And out of you she sees herself more proper
> Than any of her lineaments can show her.
>
> (III. v. 54–6)

The mirror image, as usual, signals a context where the relation between the subject and the external world is in doubt.

It is important to notice that Rosalind and Orlando are not excepted from this subjectivity, from the limits of their own selves. Rosalind may pronounce her opinion after Silvius, but she is no more right than he is. Orlando may not play the cult-lover quite as Silvius does, but he does write some very silly sonnets, and, even though Rosalind may think he is not a conventional lover, Jaques clearly thinks that he is. And Rosalind, when enumerating the conventional attributes he lacks to be a lover, draws attention to a different way in which Orlando is circumscribed by his own self. Instead of exhibiting the conventional 'careless desolation' in his appearance, she tells him, 'you are rather point-device in your accoutrements, as loving yourself than seeming the lover of any other' (III. ii. 354–5). Like Venus, the lover who 'looks babies' in her lover's eyes, Orlando is accused of loving his own image in Rosalind.[13]

In this sense, the forest becomes an image of the mind very directly, showing each his own image, 'constant in its imaginary character and changeable in each contact with a separate imagination'.[14] 'It appears', according to another critic, 'alternately as an idyllic "golden world" and as a harsh "desert inaccessible", mirroring the disposition of the beholder.'[15] It is a place as fluid as the world of the Sonnets or of *Richard II*, demonstrating that all reality is relative. Audrey and William are no more real than Silvius and Phebe; spontaneous idiocy is not inherently more real or even more common than affectation. Even the words one might use to try to distinguish between them are necessarily subjective in meaning, as L. C. Knights has noted: 'natural' can mean '*either* "adequately human" *or* "close down to the life of instinct" ' and 'civilised' can mean '*either* "well nurtured" *or* "artificial" '.[16]

Shakespeare's own contemporaries were equally well aware of this fluidity in the relation between the world and the self. Cervantes showed it through the 'madness' of Don Quixote; Donne made it explicit in the last lines of 'The Progress of the Soul':

> There's nothing simply good, nor ill alone,
> Of every quality comparison,
> The only measure is, and judge, opinion;[17]

and Montaigne was obsessed by it: 'Constancy it selfe is nothing but a languishing and wavering dance. I cannot settle my object; it goeth so unquietly and staggering, with a naturall drunkennesse. I take it in this plight, as it is at th'instant I ammuse my selfe about it.'[18]

The concern of *As You Like It* to demonstrate the subjective and relative nature of reality, and to allow for the subjective and relative response of each member of the audience prevents it from adopting a moral or judgemental approach to its characters, or at least from restricting itself to any single moral judgement. Unlike *Richard III*, where the framework of the play stands as a norm by which Richard can be judged, an inclusive, social norm, *As You Like It* does not present society as a collective with shared standards of judgement by which the deviant individual can be measured in this way. It emphasises instead the way society is composed of a series of individuals, all of whom are bound in by their own subjective point of view, and offers us a range of judgements. Even those characters who stand apart in some way, and seem to offer some kind of norm, characters such as Rosalind, Touchstone and Jaques, are undercut as norms by each other's existence, since no one of them can then stand as *the* norm.

Since the play has a comic structure, one might expect it to celebrate an essentially social norm, and to a certain extent it does do this in ending with the multiple marriage feast and the mass return to the city after re-ordering. But the difficulty in accepting this as the norm by which all else should be judged is Jaques, who refuses to be wholly absorbed into such a judgement. He is not condemned as a moral and social outlaw like Don John in *Much Ado* or like Richard III, but begged to stay with society at the end. What is it about Jaques that makes the regrouping society feel his loss so strongly? There is no doubt that there is much in his solitude to be condemned from the social perspective. Aristotle's condemnation is called to mind by the Duke's remark:

> I think he be transform'd into a beast;
> For I can nowhere find him like a man.   (II. vii. 1–2)

He refuses to involve himself in society or its propagation, remaining proud and self-involved, and noted by the Duke to be a libertine, threatening the comic ideals of fertility. His sexuality is sterile and corrupt, as the Duke reminds him when he turns critic:

> Most mischievous foul sin, in chiding sin;
> For thou thyself hast been a libertine,
> As sensual as the brutish sting itself;
> And all th'embossed sores and headed evils
> That thou with licence of free foot hast caught
> Wouldst thou disgorge into the general world.
>   (II. vii. 64–9)

Jaques voluntarily cuts himself off from social laws, and in his aspiration towards self-definition he is reminiscent of Richard III and the machiavellian villains. And like the boy of the Sonnets, he cultivates 'singularity', striving to emphasise his distinction and separateness from other men rather than any shared human qualities. His cult of solitude and melancholy is a way of emphasising his distinctness, and the deliberateness of the affectation is highlighted by Jaques' own self-consciousness. He incessantly draws attention to his own pose, freely admitting to its self-willed quality: 'I can suck melancholy out of a song, as a weasel sucks eggs. More, I prithee, more' (II. v. 11–13). He insists on the individuality of his melancholy, refusing to be absorbed even by a cult which would establish him as part of a group. His melancholy, he says, 'is a melancholy of mine own, compounded of many simples, extracted from many objects, and, indeed, the sundry contemplation of my travels; in which my often rumination wraps me in a most humorous sadness' (IV. i. 14–18).

Jaques exhibits precisely the characteristic self-contradiction inherent in the Elizabethan cult of solitude as a whole, that is, the presentation of this cult of the private, uncommunicated self through exaggerated public display, which then links each solitary to a group who share these solitary tendencies. And self-contradiction is in itself a recognised characteristic of the malcontent. He is seen almost as emblematic of self-division, mirroring his attempt to divide himself from society, his natural context. Marston describes the malcontent in the play of that name thus: ' . . . the Elements struggle within him; his owne soule is at variance: (within her selfe), his speach is halter-worthy at all howers'.[19] He is a type both divided and divisive, a man at odds both with himself and with the social order, and as such a threat to the order established for the regrouping society at the end of the play. Although the others lament his departure, it is only fitting that he should go, since he is an element of chaos, out of place in any collective order, as Duke Senior says:

> If he, compact of jars, grow musical,
> We shall have shortly discord in the spheres.
> (II. vii. 5–6)

In terms of the social perspective Jaques is meaningless, a part severed from the whole, from the relationships which would give it purpose. Despite his own inner awareness of his uniqueness and singularity, Jaques is a mere type to the others, and shares qualities, even down to the sense of uniqueness, with all the other solitary individuals so far described. Society slots him into the melancholy group, and characters use his label rather than his name as a mode of address, or refer to him in the third person with the label as prefix, 'melancholy Jaques' (II. i. 26, 41). The same image, the image of the mirror, relates his self-involved detachment from society to that of any solitary. It occurs in conversation with Orlando:

> *Jaq.* By my troth, I was seeking for a fool when I found you.
> *Orl.* He is drown'd in the brook; look but in, and you shall see him.
> *Jaq.* There shall I see mine own figure.
> *Orl.* Which I take to be either a fool or a cipher.
> (III. ii. 268–73)

Orlando's reply makes two points: it condemns Jaques's stance as meaningless, by calling him a 'cipher', and it links it with the similar detachment of the professional fool. Both Jaques and Touchstone stand apart from the social group and from the dramatic structure, and as such their perspective is different from that within the group. They see the social order with a more critical eye than those who are immersed in it, and their own reality is more static than the reality of those who engage fully in relationships and adapt accordingly. It is in fact Jaques's refusal to accept the conventions of social decorum, and adapt his nature to time, place and person, that leads the other characters to classify him as a type and to find him simultaneously amusing and socially unacceptable. The fool is more acceptable because he masks his criticism behind the mask of folly, which appears to integrate him into society, but in fact preserves his detachment by concealing his true identity. As the Duke remarks, 'he uses his folly like a stalking horse, and under the presentation of that he shoots his wit' (v. iv. 100–1).

The relationship between the fool and the malcontent is not a relationship in the same sense as the other relationships in the play. First, only Jaques is aware of it, and second, his awareness is a purely cerebral recognition of kinship, not a feeling of affection for the fool as an individual. He simply sees that they are linked by a common alienation, cynicism and self-awareness. They are both at odds with the world and with themselves, both presenting the world with a contrived social self which protects their inner selves from becoming committed in any way. It is into these two outsiders that the self-divided personality of tragedy passes. In the artificial world of comedy, where division among characters is more central than inner division of the individual, which is not explored in the same depth as in tragedy, Jaques and Touchstone become emblematic of division, and thus exist on a different level from the other characters by virtue of their symbolic role. They 'express the conscience of a divided world, not by being the victims of its tensions, but by expressing those tensions in their own characters'.[20]

Although individually self-divided, the fool and the malcontent are also like the two halves of a single self, and seem to complete one another.[21] Both derive elements from the same single medieval figure, the Vice, who combined the characteristics of devilry, foolery, wit and villainy in himself, though of course both have sources elsewhere too. Jaques expresses his sense of incompleteness by constantly seeking out of the fool and by emulating him. He is literally looking for the fool when Orlando tells him to look in the brook, reminding him that the fool is also a part of himself. He explicitly states his longing to become a professional fool:

O noble fool!
A worthy fool! Motley's the only wear . . .
O that I were a fool!
I am ambitious for a motley coat.

(II. vii. 33–4, 42–3)

He recognises a similarity in their purpose in standing critically
aloof, to 'Cleanse the foul body of th'infected world' (II. vii. 60), and
envies the protection the fool gives himself by phrasing his criticism
in 'mangled forms' (42). He considers the fool to be 'deep
contemplative' (31) like himself, and the fool is the only one who
can crack Jaques's mask of melancholy and make him laugh.

Jaques cannot then be judged simply from society's perspective as
an outsider, an anarchic threat to the social and moral order, since
in standing outside society, he also in some sense stands above it,
seeing it more clearly than it sees itself. As an observer outside the
framework of social commitment, he mocks those within it, and is
even allowed the last word sometimes. He questions the means by
which society prepares its feasts, the climactic expression of the
collective ideal, by lamenting the slaying of the deer and condemning the courtiers who have invaded the forest as 'mere usurpers,
tyrants' who kill animals even 'In their assign'd and native
dwelling-place' (II. i. 61, 63). Although the First Lord's account of
the spectacle of Jaques weeping beside the weeping deer is
undeniably funny, which prevents us from taking Jaques's criticism
as an absolute, it none the less registers a criticism of society.[22]
Following on immediately after the Duke's conventional speech in
praise of the pastoral idyll, the irony cannot be mistaken, since the
Duke's speech implies a life which imitates the ideals of the golden
age, whereas Jaques's condemnation of killing for food draws
attention to one of the familiar signs which signalled the end of the
golden age, a time when, according to Ovid, grain grew of its own
accord and men ate only the fruits of the earth. Killing for food was
a clear falling off from the ideal, and in that sense Jaques's
condemnation is justified, if exaggerated and egotistically
presented.

Jaques's mockery is allowed to resound *after* the communal song
praising the moral superiority of the pastoral life. Mimicking the
form of that song, Jaques sings a cynical reversal (quoted on p. 97
above), and when Amiens questions him innocently about the
unfamiliar word 'ducdame', Jaques carries the mockery a stage

further by turning to the group assembled round him to explain, ' 'Tis a Greek invocation, to call fools into a circle' (l. 55). Yet even this is primarily humorous and is as much a comment on Jacques's cynicism as on the naiveté of pastoral ideals and comic fellowship. Only Jaques's final summing up can be taken in any sense as a norm, because the satirical tone is absent and it is a speech which recognises the qualities of each individual with judicious balance. The placing of Jaques's farewell, at the end of this reasoned assessment and before the celebratory dance anticipating the return to social order, gives it both prominence and value:

> So to your pleasures;
> I am for other than for dancing measures.
>
> (v. iv. 186–7)

It is unaggressive enough not to upset the comic order, yet serious enough in tone to pose a question as to whether the social order is the only right and significant context for the individual. The celebration of the social ideal in the final dance is necessarily qualified, though not disordered, by Jaques's refusal to participate and the regret it engenders among the others. The ending of the play neither resolutely condemns the solitary, like *Richard III*, nor implies that solitude is a kind of death, like *Richard II*. It allows the inner life of the solitary to co-exist with the external perspective of the community, so that neither one totally denies the validity of the alternative way, but the two are not reconciled. The play shows both ways, the solitary and the social, both from their own and from each other's perspective. It ends, like the typical Elizabethan debate on solitude, with an explicit conclusion which favours society, but a qualification sanctioning solitude which is as resonant as the supposed conclusion. Despite the full stop of affirmation, the question mark remains.

8 'The heart of my mystery': *Hamlet*

In *Hamlet*, the outsider becomes, both structurally and morally, the hero of the play. Solitude, which has been linked thus far in Shakespeare's work with atheism, amorality, narcissism and affectation, and only hesitantly with more admirable qualities,[1] now comes to seem, if only temporarily, the inevitable state of the man who values the inner life and truth to self above all else. Yet to determine whether Hamlet is a natural, voluntary solitary is more problematical than with earlier solitaries. There is much in the play to suggest that he has been a sociable, spontaneous man: his welcome of Rosencrantz and Guildenstern is a recognition of past fellowship and trust, and his continuing friendship with Horatio confirms his need for company and for a relationship of mutual trust. The Hamlet whom Ophelia remembers as 'th'observ'd of all observers' (III. i. 154), whom Gertrude finds 'too much changed' (II. ii. 36), in whom even Claudius can see that 'nor th' exterior nor the inward man / Resembles that it was' (II. ii. 6–7), was clearly less mystifying and withdrawn than the one they see in the play. Hamlet himself is unhappy with the isolation into which he is forced by his father's death, his mother's 'o'erhasty marriage' (II. ii. 57) and the imposed task of revenge, so alien to his nature. His pleasure in seeing Rosencrantz and Guildenstern, his warm welcome of the players, his reliance on Horatio, reveal not unsociability but loneliness.

But Hamlet has become a cult-figure for every kind of alienation in the ages following his own, which suggests that audiences, despite all references within the play to a sociable nature, perceive Hamlet's solitude as his most striking feature. And Hamlet's possession of all the causes and characteristics of Elizabethan cult-solitude (melancholy, travel, study, grief, rejected love, general discontent and world-weariness) suggest too that he was regarded as an archetypal solitary in his own age. If both Jaques and Hamlet are taken as pointing to an Elizabethan cult of solitude, then Shakespeare mocks through Jaques the fashionable courtiers who cultivated the affectations, and identifies through Hamlet with the genuine and involuntary sense of alienation and loneliness in which the cult of solitude originated. Certainly Hamlet's solitariness is the first thing any audience must notice on seeing the play performed. The first scene in which Hamlet appears (Act I, Scene ii) presents in strongly visual terms the isolation which is depicted in more complexity in his soliloquies. Hamlet is dressed in 'solemn black' (I. ii. 78), and this singles him out from the rest of the court, who presumably are no longer in mourning, since Hamlet is criticised for his excess in mourning so long. Despite the explicit reason for black, the cult-association of black with the malcontent, and the melancholy humour in general, would not have gone unnoticed by an Elizabethan audience. Hamlet sits apart from the rest of the court, his silence emblematic of his solitude. When he does speak, he does not use words to communicate, to engage himself with those around him, but to seal himself off even further. He speaks more to himself than to the King, who addresses him, and adopts the Vice's characteristic of speaking in an aside with a double meaning: 'A little more than kin, and less than kind' (65); 'I am too much in the sun' (67). He insists on the incommunicability of his inner self, jealously guarding 'that within which passes show' (85), thus insisting simultaneously on the division between his private and his public self.

The contrast between his short, uncommunicative answers in reply to public questions and his outpouring of himself in soliloquy at the end of the scene establishes soliloquy as his natural medium, another characteristic previously associated with the Vice, who also reveals his true self only in soliloquy and aside. Despite the references to a Hamlet once sanguine, it is impossible to believe that soliloquy, or introspection, has not always been part of his nature. Throughout the scene he has deliberately held himself aloof; throughout the play he will demonstrate his difficulty in committing himself to any public gesture, in engaging himself, a difficulty to which Montaigne also confesses, in a way that is again symptomatic of the time: 'I engage myself with difficulty. As much as I can, I employ my selfe wholly to my selfe.'[2] Hamlet is clearly a natural solitary in this respect, delighting in his own inwardness, cherishing his uncommunicated and unique self, valuing most highly those elements in his nature which are private. His self-awareness and introspectiveness are not characteristics developed purely by recent

mortified by recent events

events, but part of his nature. His intense awareness of the inner depth of his existence, 'my heart's core . . . my heart of heart' (III. ii. 71), his sense of outrage that Rosencrantz and Guildenstern should presume to 'pluck out the heart of my mystery' (III. ii. 356–7) are directly comparable with Petrarch's 'Secretum meum mihi', the refusal to engage in society totally, or to be measured and judged by external, social contexts. It is this same egoism, this aspiration towards self-definition, which characterised Richard III, and which was singled out by Shakespeare's contemporaries as a cause of the breakdown of relationships and hence of society as a whole. Donne's lament for the disintegration of society (quoted on p. 37 above) is only the beginning of a diatribe which singles out the individual worship of the inward mystery as the destroyer of social bonds which link the self to the world outside itself:

> 'Tis all in pieces, all coherence gone;
> All just supply, and all relation:
> Prince, subject, father, son, are things forgot,
> For every man alone thinks he hath got
> To be a phoenix, and that then can be
> None of that kind, of which he is, but he.[3]

Hamlet feels impelled to follow his own nature, erecting that into his first principle, yet he is also struggling to follow a collective, social ethic, one that is alien to his nature, the ethic of revenge. His desire to be true to himself conflicts with his sense of duty to his bond; his refusal to commit himself in company conflicts with a need to fulfil commitments and acknowledge the humanity he shares with his fellow men. In his torment he exemplifies the paradox around which the debate on solitude centred and which one critic has desribed as 'Shakespeare's perennial concern: man forever bound, forever desiring his freedom, and yet finding true happiness and fulfilment only in acknowledging the bondage which links him to other men'.[4]

Polonius's advice to Laertes:

> to thine own self be true,
> And it must follow, as the night the day,
> Thou canst not then be false to any man.

> (I. iii. 78–80)

is often quoted approvingly out of context and often restricted to the first line, as though Shakespeare, through Polonius, preached the doctrine of truth to self as the individual's primary concern. Yet this is not what Polonius advises. He advises truth to self as a way of being true to society, not as a virtue in itself, and certainly not as a virtue alternative to the duty to society. The occurrence of the same advice in another context makes this point even clearer. Bacon, in his essay 'Of Wisdom for a Man's Self', says this:

> An ant is a wise creature for itself, but it is a shrewd thing in an orchard or garden. And certainly men that are great lovers of themselves waste the public. Divide with reason between self-love and society; and be so true to thyself, as thou be not false to others; specially to thy king and country. It is a poor centre of a man's actions, *himself*. It is right earth. For that only stands fast upon his own centre; whereas all things that have affinity with the heavens, move upon the centre of another, which they benefit.[5]

It is possible that Bacon is borrowing from Shakespeare here, or that the phrase was simply a piece of proverbial wisdom, which is after all the staple of Polonius's speech. The very fact that the advice comes from Polonius should serve as a caution against taking it as a creed for Hamlet. It seems rather to be a piece of advice which Shakespeare puts into Polonius's mouth only to question it, since it proves to be quite the opposite of what Hamlet finds. Hamlet, following the first part of the maxim by being true to himself, finds that he is forced to be false to others, if he is to retain his integrity in a false society. The only justification for the anti-social stance he adopts is that he is trying to be true to himself. In order to keep his inner self pure and free from the corruption that surrounds him he becomes as cunning a dissembler as Richard III, using the same techniques of wordplay and assumed roles, and reserving his true self for solitude. His refusal to frame himself in the normal dramatic modes of communication and relationship is a refusal to be defined by a social context. Yet unlike Richard III, his principle of truth to self at the expense of truth to society seems admirable in the circumstances, and morally superior to the alternative of engaging himself in such a society.

Nevertheless, *Hamlet* does not offer this way as an ideal. It is simply a necessity in a society as degenerate as the one in which Hamlet finds himself. But Hamlet himself experiences the limitations of such an existence, which confines itself to the inner world and fobs off the external world with mere shows. Trying to protect his integrity by remaining self-enclosed, he finds that integrity, in the root sense of 'wholeness' or unity of being, is exactly what evades him so long as he is an incomplete being in this way, severed from social involvement. In an illuminating essay on *Hamlet*, which takes the phrase, 'to say "one"' (v. ii. 74) as a 'metaphor' for the meaning of the play, Ralph Berry has argued that the recurrence of the number 'one' in Hamlet's language is a mark of his search for wholeness, a wholeness which he does not find until the last scene, where he performs a social act, an act of public commitment, in killing the King. Berry writes:

> 'One' is of all numbers the most resonant. It bears the implications of unity and self-hood, and it has moreover a significant past in *Hamlet*. Is not Hamlet saying that man's life is a quest for unity, for the oneness of self and situation? And is not the final scene the statement of a profound accord between self and situation, action and awareness?[6]

But 'one' also has associations with solitude and singularity, the sense of uniqueness and of apartness explored through the repetitions of the word 'single' in the Sonnets. 'One', ironically, acts as both the ideal Hamlet seeks and the reason for his failure to achieve it. It represents the unified self he longs to be and the isolation from society, the severing of natural context, which prevents him from being a complete man.

Northrop Frye writes: 'In Shakespearean tragedy, man is not really man until he has entered what is called a social contract, when he ceases to be a "subject" in the philosophical sense and becomes a subject in the political one, essentially related to his society,'[7] and Shakespeare voices very similar sentiments explicitly in *Troilus and Cressida*:

> no man is the lord of anything,
> Though in and of him there be much consisting,
> Till he communicate his parts to others;
> Nor doth he of himself know them for aught
> Till he behold them formed in th'applause
> Where th'are extended;[8]   (III. iii. 115–20)

It is not until the last scene that Hamlet makes this commitment, or contract, and enters into a relation with his society. Throughout the rest of the play he involves himself wholly in his existence as a philosophical subject, isolating himself within his own over-active self-awareness. Frye elsewhere points out, with reference to Richard III, that 'for a philosopher, isolation is the first act of consciousness',[9] and it is in this primary isolation of self-consciousness that Hamlet remains until the last scene. His speech is on a more inward level than that of normal communication and confuses even those closest to him:

> *Ham.* My father—methinks I see my father.
> *Hor.* Where, my lord?
> *Ham.* In my mind's eye, Horatio.   (I. ii. 183–5)

He is only too aware of the imprisonment of the individual within the limits of his own perspective, and distinguishes openly between the world as it is and as he sees it. He knows that there is beauty in the external world, but to him it is merely 'a foul and pestilent congregation of vapours' (II. ii. 301–2). He knows that 'there is nothing either good or bad, but thinking makes it so' (II. ii. 248–9),[10] but the knowledge does not help him to escape from the prison of his way of thinking. Physical space becomes insignificant by comparison with the space of the inner world, which taints the whole of the physical world with its viewpoint, so that the whole world becomes an image of the prison within the mind. Hamlet explicitly says that Denmark is a prison to him (II. ii. 250), acknowledging with full consciousness that the real prison is in the mind: 'O God, I could be bounded in a nutshell and count myself a king of infinite space, were it not that I have bad dreams' (II. ii. 253–5).

The mirror, so strongly associated with the solitude and self-division of the inward self, is incorporated into the structure rather than the language of this play. (It does of course also take material shape in Gertrude's self-examination, where the parallels with *Richard II* are obvious.) Hamlet's solitude is mirrored in the various forms of isolation about him: Ophelia, sealed off in the world of her own madness; Claudius, isolated by guilt and the fear of damnation; Gertrude, again torn by guilt and punished by Hamlet's rejection; Laertes, with a father dead, a sister mad, and at the mercy of Claudius' clever schemes. Fortinbras too has a father dead, and in this respect both he and Laertes mirror Hamlet's situation. Hamlet sees mirror-images all around him: Ophelia's betrayal of him (in his terms) is the crueller for being an image of Gertrude's; Claudius's attempts to be kind and fatherly to Hamlet are an ironical image of the true father, who also has a reflection in the ghost. Hamlet even helps to create reflections of his situation by requesting the extract of Trojan tragedy which leads him to compare his apathy with the actor's passion, and by setting up the play-within-the play and its dumb show.[11] These structural mirrors in fact become a hallmark of Shakespearean tragedy generally, emphasising the hero's vision of the whole world as an image of self and yet showing ironically how, despite the individual's feeling of uniqueness and isolation, he is in fact not alone in his situation, but more like other men than he thinks.

As in the Sonnets and *As You Like It*, extreme self-awareness reduces the world to a mere relative contingent upon the self. It is small wonder that Hamlet finds it difficult to act in accordance with collective norms and values, since he does not accept them as absolutes. He is himself his only absolute, and as such is free to remould himself as he likes from moment to moment. To some extent this is as Hamlet says 'an antic disposition' (I. v. 172) deliberately adopted to delude those around him; but it is impossible to resist the idea that the assumed madness is merely a way of justifying a fluidity which exists spontaneously in Hamlet's nature. With his highly-developed awareness of subjectivity and hence of the relativity of his personal experience of the world, it is surely a natural as well as a calculated response on his part to experiment with different selves. He is not committed to society in any way, and has no reason to try to maintain a stable ego to affirm any such commitment; in his detachment he is free to adopt any role he chooses without violating the absolute within, which he keeps apart from all his public displays in any case. Given his perception that the world is fluid rather than static, relative rather than absolute, it is understandable that his response to it should also be fluid and experimental. As for Richard III, if for different reasons, the world of the play is something of a play to him, and this relationship with the world around him sets him structurally apart from it. Hamlet treats the play like a play-within-a-play, a testing ground for different roles, and in this respect makes yet another of the Vice's characteristics more morally acceptable. His detachment from society, his lack of commitment to its values, is expressed through the formal metaphor of his detachment from the play. His topical references to the Elizabethan world outside the play (to the boy-actors, for example), his discourse on methods of acting, his devising of an actual play-within-the-play, his deliberate assumption of false masks in public, all set him apart from the world in which the other characters are fully involved. His aloofness from the dramatic form and his refusal to express himself fully through it is the logical structural corollary of his first outburst against Gertrude's use of the word 'seems' in connection with him, an outburst which is really a complaint that the Danish court provides no forms which would express him, no ' "objective correlative" '[12] for his inner state.

Hamlet's preoccupation with the discrepancy between the complexity of the inner self and the inadequacy of the public images through which it can be presented, the dissatisfaction which leads him to experiment with different masks in presenting an image to society, can be seen in the frequency with which the word 'form' is repeated.[13] The word draws attention to the same longing as does the word 'one', the longing for unity between thought and action, between private self and public action. Ophelia implies that there was a time when they were one, when Hamlet was 'The glass of fashion and the mould of form . . . That unmatch'd form and feature of blown youth' (III. i. 153, 159). Even Claudius speaks of Hamlet's 'transformation' (II. ii. 5), and both he and Gertrude describe the present Hamlet in terms of division rather than unity, talking of the 'exterior' and the 'inward' man as separate entities. Hamlet's own admiration for unity of form and substance is clearly expressed in his praise of his father as

> A combination and a form indeed
> Where every god did seem to set his seal,
> To give the world assurance of a man,   (III. v. 60–2)

and in his praising of both inward capacity and outward form in the human race as a whole: 'What a piece of work is a man! How noble in reason! how infinite in faculties! in form and moving, how express and admirable!' (II. ii. 302–4).

But Hamlet, on being forced through his father's murder and his mother's remarriage to see how corrupt is the society in which he lives, becomes divided, deliberately cultivating a gap between thought and deed. And so jealously does he guard his inner life, so intensely does he limit his existence to the confines of his own mind, that action of any kind becomes an increasingly difficult commitment, since it involves engagement of the self in society on its own ground. In a sense, the play can also be viewed as a continuation of the familiar debate on the relative merits of action and contemplation, already posed by Shakespeare in *As You Like It.* Hamlet, once a well-balanced fusion of action and contemplation, courtier, soldier and scholar is faced at the beginning of the play with an oath that commits him to action just at the point where circumstances have heightened his contemplative faculties to the point where he has withdrawn from society into the world of the inner self. The struggle embodied in the play is then the attempt to bridge that gap. Hamlet himself explicitly blames his inaction on his heightened contemplative activity ('some craven scruple / Of thinking too precisely on th'event' (IV. iv. 40–1). It is 'conscience',[14] he recognises, that 'does make cowards of us all' (III. i. 83). So confined within the limits of mental space is he that he cannot even conceive of action except in terms of thought. When the ghost first issues the command to revenge, for example, Hamlet vows to fulfil it

> with wings as swift
> As meditation or the thoughts of love (I. v. 29–30)

and by the end of Act IV he is still renewing his vow in similarly ironical and self-defeating terms:

> O, from this time forth,
> My thoughts be bloody, or be nothing worth!
> (IV. iv. 65–6)

It is the public commitment inherent in action which Hamlet finds difficult. His sense that all his public gestures are merely role-playing prevents him from making such a gesture into a commitment of his private self. Hamlet feels too that his inability to act makes him somehow less than a man, and in one sense this is true. Shakespeare's plays from *Hamlet* onwards strive towards the definition of man, but distinguish clearly between manhood in the traditional sexist terms, meaning strength, or even brutality, and manhood meaning humanity, which may resemble weakness in the eyes of those who set store by the first definition of a man. Hamlet thinks he is unmanly because he is weak, but the real sense in which he fails as a man is in being incomplete, in allowing his inner world to become a substitute for social participation. Characteristically, his own definition of man (except in the praise quoted on p. 114 above, where he applauds the combination of inner and outer faculties) emphasises the inward qualities in splendid isolation:

> What is a man,
> If his chief good and market of his time
> Be but to sleep and feed? A beast, no more!
> Sure he that made us with such large discourse,
> Looking before and after, gave us not
> That capability and godlike reason
> To fust in us unus'd.   (IV. iv. 33–9)

Not that he is wrong in what he says; it is just inadequate, in that it makes no mention of man as a social being, and implies by this omission that a man can be defined wholly in terms of himself, without reference to the world in which he is placed.

The play as a whole repeatedly desecrates the social bonds which create order. The King, who should be the figure of order in the commonwealth, is in fact a source of disorder and corruption. The harmony between inner order in the individual man and the greater order of the universe is perverted into a mutual disorder, a sterile garden. Life itself is violently and unnaturally cut off. Bonds of love, kinship and loyalty are violated by incest, betrayal and murder. And Hamlet, despite his rejection of social involvement, understands something of the social ideal. He detaches himself as a response to the perverted nature of his particular society, but he struggles throughout the play to uphold that one bond between father and son which remains from the days of social order, and the breaking of which is so often cited by Shakespeare and his contemporaries as emblematic of universal anarchy. Hamlet retains his humanity by clinging to this one bond which preserves him from total solitude and self-enclosure, and which he finally overcomes his solitude to fulfil.

Hamlet's treatment of the bond between word and truth follows a similar pattern. From being one who is by nature sincere (his first expression of outrage against the word 'seems' suggests a man of integrity), he becomes a dissembler, voluntarily detaching words from truth, and finally returns to an insistence on restoring the bond between word and truth. After his initial rejection of hypocrisy in words, he shows in deeds and in silence how little of his true self he does now communicate to society. Language, the medium of communication, becomes, as in the Sonnets and *Richard II*, a way of reinforcing the barriers around the self, and of fending off intruders.[15] Montaigne describes very clearly the social and moral significance of the word:

> Our intelligence being onely conducted by the way of the Word: Who so falsifieth the same, betraieth publik society. It is the onely instrument, by meanes whereof our wils and thoughts are communicated: it is the interpretour of our soules: If that faile us we hold our selves no more, we enter-know one another no longer. If it deceive us, it breaketh al our commerce, and dissolveth al bonds of our policie.[16]

Hamlet's manipulations and games with words are overtly anti-social, confirming his detachment from social concerns. The value of words in this play is summed up in the empty resonance of Hamlet's reply to Polonius:

> *Pol.* What do you read, my lord?
> *Ham.* Words, words, words,   (II. ii. 190–1)

which clearly implies the separation between words and meaning, the way in which words, like individual men, can be rendered meaningless by being cut off from any context which would explain their significance. Hamlet deliberately uses words to prevent, rather than to enable, communication, and delights in confusing his audience:

> *Ros.* I understand you not, my lord.
> *Ham.* I am glad of it.   (IV. ii. 21–2)

Only at the end does he return to a desire for words to be linked with truth. Although for him 'the rest is silence' (v. ii. 350), a blessed escape from hypocrisies and the fluidity of words, his last request is that Horatio should survive to tell his story. Like the seventeenth-century autobiographers, although withdrawing from the world, he is concerned that the truth about him should be finally communicated to the world he has rejected.

The violation of the bond between word and truth is the image of the universal violation of collective absolutes in the play. The moral absolutes which should define and justify society—justice, honesty, order, reverence for bonds—deteriorate into the subjective values placed on them by each individual. The loss of any absolute sense in words, so much are they manipulated and distorted, mirrors the loss of any absolute value in anything. 'For Hamlet', as another critic has written, 'the dilemma is the difficulty of forming absolute values based upon absolute truth in a world where absolute truth is inaccessible.'[17] Hamlet's own heightened subjectivity and scepticism eat at the root of all absolute collective values.

Shakespeare seems divided in *Hamlet* between admiration for the inward solitude which Hamlet so proudly defends in a false society, and condemnation of the individualism to which the disintegration of social values is linked in the first place. The division arises partly out of Shakespeare's refusal to judge in this play: he portrays a degenerate society and the withdrawal from it of one individual, but he does not, as in *Richard III*, suggest which comes first. Although individual solitude and the decay of society are closely linked in all Shakespeare's work, and generally in the writings of his contemporaries, the decision as to which is cause and which effect becomes increasingly difficult to make. What is clear is that, however heroic we may judge Hamlet's solitude to be under the circumstances, it is neither right nor desirable in absolute terms. Hamlet's solitude is the source simultaneously of his nobility and of his tragedy. Although his solitude is justifiable, it deprives him of the only context in which he could achieve total self-fulfilment.

9 'We two alone': *King Lear*

King Lear is, from the first scene, a play of solitaries. Cordelia's stubbornness earns her rejection and exile; Kent is banished; Edgar is forced to flee in the most lonely of all disguises, as a Bedlam beggar. But solitude goes against their natures; they are unwillingly solitary, and throughout the play they attempt to heal the broken bonds by which they have been cut off. Edmund, the self-willed, 'natural' solitary, reverts to the role of villain, as in *Richard III*. Lear himself initiates his own isolation by retiring from his public role and responsibility as king, and after this voluntary act becomes increasingly cut off from society by the chain of events which it sets in motion. E. A. J. Honigmann has described Lear's progressive withdrawal with poignant emphasis:

> . . . he rushes away from Goneril ('Away, away!' I. iv. 289), retreats into the storm, escapes Cordelia (IV. iv. 1), runs away from the Gentleman (IV. vi. 205), and finally looks forward to prison, where he and Cordelia can withdraw for good . . . And when things go badly for him he retires into the inner self, where no one can follow . . . Torn open by grief and rage, pitifully exposed by madness, the quintessential Lear shrinks into a secret place and wards off the prying world with his characteristic verbal gesture, negation.[1]

Although I think Honigmann is wrong to see in Lear's looking forward to prison with Cordelia a culmination of his withdrawal, as this chapter will argue, the description is in every other way true to the characteristic movement of the play towards inwardness and isolation.

Yet although the actuality depicted everywhere in the play is this movement towards solitude, the motivation, the movement in values, is towards the medieval ideal of social unity based on mutual

obligation and loyalty, the acknowledgement of bonds. In this way
the play moves against the general shift in values of its times in its
celebration of society as the natural fulfilment of both duty and
desire. *King Lear* returns to the strongly judgemental perspective of
Richard III in its affirmation of the social bond as a bond of nature,
too strong to be severed by individual will. 'Existence is tragic in
King Lear because existence is inseparable from relation; we are born
from and to it.'[2] The play is an indictment of the solitary impulse
and its destructive effect on the bonds between men. It portrays
willing solitude as an evil and unwilling solitude as the worst form of
suffering: 'Who alone suffers suffers most i'th'mind' (III. vi. 104).
The central scenes on the heath show the sufferings of four solitaries
alleviated by the comfort they offer one another simply by keeping
company.

Frequent parallels between *King Lear* and medieval writings
confirm its adherence to the traditional social ideal. Lear's concern
for his fool and his hundred knights, his protectiveness towards those
who serve him, echoes the values described by Malory as prevailing
at Arthur's court, remembered fondly by the Wanderer in the Old
English lyric, or described explicitly as here by John of Salisbury:
'. . . inferiors owe it to their superiors to provide them with service,
just as the superiors in their turn owe it to their inferiors to provide
them with all things needful for their protection and succor.'[3] The
loyalty of Kent and the Fool shows their respect for this same social
order. Men are judged in this play by how well they fulfil their
appointed place in society, or, to paraphrase Cordelia, according to
their bonds. Judgement according to any other criterion is usually
an indication of the speaker's own depravity. Oswald's flouting of
the established order in describing Lear as 'my lady's father' (I. iv.
78) should be judged alongside Kent's description of him as:

> Royal Lear,
> Whom I have ever honour'd as my king,
> Lov'd as my father, as my master follow'd,
> As my great patron thought on in my prayers.
>
> (I. i. 138–41)

Oswald's defiance of the natural social order is symptomatic of
the desecration of the old order by the self-interested, those who
value their private good higher than the common weal, Goneril,
Regan and Edmund. Their attempts to bring down the old feudal

order take physical shape in their gradual paring of Lear's train, the emblem of his authority and his capacity as protector. In stripping him of his knights, Lear's daughters are trying to strip him of his kingship and his authority, since although he has renounced it in name, he finds himself unable to renounce it in nature. Like the true king described in Chapter 5 above, kingship for him is not an assumed role separable from the self, but inherent in it. One of Lear's supposedly riotous knights makes this new disrespect towards Lear painfully explicit:

> . . . to my judgment, your Highness is not entertain'd with that ceremonious affection as you were wont; there's a great abatement of kindness appears as well in the general dependants as in the Duke himself also and your daughter. (I. iv. 57–61)

But by such plain speaking the knight fulfils his duty to Lear, as Kent did in the first scene, and as Shakespeare is at pains to emphasise in the phrasing 'my duty cannot be silent when I think your Highness wrong'd' (64–5). The ideal nature of this particular master–servant relationship is highlighted by the contrasts elsewhere in the play: the sickly, fawning loyalty of Oswald to Goneril, or Cornwall's vicious murder of the servant who tries, as Kent did, to perform the duty of saving his master from folly, by warning him against injuring Gloucester.

The minute calculation of needs on which Lear's daughters base their attempts to cut down his train is in itself a contradiction of feudal values, which rest on mutual need, and on the rights and duties of a king, not on the petty reckoning of individual situations. In cutting down the symbols of an ideal with this misplaced literal-mindedness, Goneril and Regan are really aiming to destroy Lear's sense of himself as a feudal lord and to reduce him to his merely literal status, a useless old man. They repeatedly address him as such until he is humbled to the point where he describes himself in this way.

But when the play opens it is clear that Lear defines himself neither in this reductive way, nor in the individualistic way, from within the self, but by his roles and his relationships, his place in society. His obsessive repetition of the words 'king' and 'father' throughout most of the rest of the play demonstrates how strongly these self-images are rooted in him. Lear's conception of individuals as defined by their relationships is right, although he falls short in the performance. Evil defines itself in this play by the deliberateness with which it undermines relationships and works towards the isolation of each individual within his own self. This wilful destruction of bonds and cultivation of solitude necessarily threatens the very existence of society, since 'there is no *Society* found without *Bond*, nor *Bond* without *Society* . . . Wherefore the bond or duty, is no other thing then the habitude respect or custome which the associats have together, which is an impulsive beginning to labour for their common good, as their only end.'[4] Lear appeals to both bonds, the duties owed to him as King and as father, in trying to bring Regan and her husband to speak to him:

> The King would speak with Cornwall; the dear father
> Would with his daughter speak; commands their service,
>   (II. iv. 99–100)

and the evil of these two is measured in their refusal to appear, their open contempt for these bonds. Their denial of Lear's rights as king and father brings Lear to question his own identity: 'we are not ourselves' (105), a questioning which is repeatedly forced on him until he is driven mad. His hysterical obsession with these names, king, father, daughter, keeps the cause of his madness constantly displayed, as does the Fool's echoing of these same names in his rhymes. The isolation of madness itself is intensified by the loneliness inherent in its source: rejection. Rejection is the unifying pre-occupation of Lear's ravings, as of his saner laments: 'filial ingratitude' (III. iv. 14), 'unkind daughters' (70), 'discarded fathers' (71).

His daughters' rejection of their bonds lead him to question the reality of those bonds. The subject of legitimacy which obsesses Edmund mirrors the unnaturalness and uncertainty about relationships which pervades the main plot. Lear's reaction to Goneril's first open display of harshness is an incredulous question: 'Are you our daughter?' (I. iv. 217), followed by a need to disown a relationship so dishonoured: 'Degenerate bastard!' (253). Leaving Goneril as a result of her rejection of her bond, he acknowledges that if she will not behave as a daughter, he too must cease to be a father: 'I will forget my nature. So kind a father!' (I. v. 31). When he comes to Regan instead, her greeting is formal, acknowledging his role as king rather than father: 'I am glad to see your Highness' (II. iv. 126), and Lear responds to this aloofness by trying to reassure himself of the father–daughter relationship between them, again through the metaphor of legitimacy:

> Regan, I think you are; I know what reason
> I have to think so. If thou shouldst not be glad,
> I would divorce me from thy mother's tomb,
> Sepulchring an adultress.   (127–30)

It is only by having these basic bonds questioned, which he has taken for granted as natural and therefore necessarily present, that Lear comes to realise the full value of Cordelia's affirmation of love in the first scene:

> I love your Majesty
> According to my bond; no more nor less.   (I. i. 91–2)

Humiliated by the rejection of Goneril and Regan and the realisation that he has wronged Cordelia, he advances the claim of kinship far more hesitantly with her:

> Do not laugh at me;
> For, as I am a man, I think this lady
> To be my child Cordelia,   (IV. vii. 68–70)

but her simple, unhesitating affirmation, 'And so I am, I am' (70), re-states the total and absolute nature of the bond.

The flaw in Lear's conception of the bonds of society is its one-sided emphasis. He is quick to remind others of 'The offices of nature, bond of childhood, / Effects of courtesy, dues of gratitude' (II. iv. 177–8) which they owe to him, but less aware of his own obligations. Kent, Cordelia and the Fool all show themselves more unswervingly loyal to Lear than he is to them, although the fact that he shows something of loyalty to them, particularly to the Fool, makes us judge his failures as evidence of folly rather than evil. These three demonstrate the fact that the individual life only gains significance through its bonds with others, and is meaningless severed from the social context. As Kent tells Lear, individual life has value only in relation:

> My life I never held but as a pawn
> To wage against thine enemies; nor fear to lose it,
> Thy safety being motive.   (I. i. 154–6)

The life that cuts itself off from relationships and its natural bonds
will die, both spiritually and physically, as Albany tells Goneril:

> That nature which contemns it origin
> Cannot be border'd certain in itself;
> She that herself will sliver and disbranch
> From her material sap perforce must wither
> And come to deadly use.   (IV. ii. 32–6)

To Albany, Goneril is not a human being, but, like Richard III, a
monster, deformed, bestial, fiendish. There has been much conjec-
ture about what Albany means when he calls her here a 'self-cover'd
thing' (62). Kenneth Muir, in his note in the Arden edition of the
play, lists some of these, but does not include a reading which seems
to me likely in this context, that Goneril is imprisoned by her own
self-interest, disgusting to Albany simply for her unnatural involvement with self to the exclusion of all the rest of humanity, and
inhuman in her isolation.

Edmund, like Richard III, bears a physical image of his moral
deformity in that he is a bastard. The euphemism 'natural' for
'illegitimate' lends an irony to Edmund's unnatural behaviour to
his father and brother. Like Goneril, he cares only for himself,
desecrating all bonds that would make him human. He announces
his self-contained, or 'self-cover'd' stance in the familiar, defiant 'I
am': 'I should have been that I am, had the maidenliest star in the
firmament twinkled on my bastardizing' (I. ii. 125–7). His bastardy
is emblematic of his denial of all bonds, a denial shown at its most
corrupt in Edmund's willingness to exploit the emotive power of the
bond in order to sever bonds. He incenses Gloucester against his
legitimate son, Edgar, by forging a letter, feigning loyalty to Edgar
as a reason for not showing the letter at first, and finally driving in
the wedge between legitimate father and son by recounting to
Gloucester how he tried to dissuade his brother from parricide by
reminding him 'with how manifold and strong a bond / The child
was bound to th'father' (II. i. 47–8). In the same way he manipulates
Edgar into giving the appearance of guilt by fleeing, with
professions of love and constant reminders of the bond between
them in his repetition of the word 'brother' as a form of address.

The bonds that Goneril, Regan, Edmund and their associates do
uphold are cruel parodies of the true bonds, and only confirm the
real isolation of self-love. Goneril's contempt for Albany, her

adultery and her abuse of him, and Regan's partnership in sadism with Cornwall, again simultaneous with adultery, provide a sinister reversal of Cordelia's obedience to France, and their inverted relationships with their husbands are anticipated in Cordelia's initial denouncement of their falseness in proclaiming love for Lear:

> Why have my sisters husbands, if they say
> They love you all? Haply, when I shall wed,
> That lord whose hand must take my plight shall carry
> Half my love with him, half my care and duty.
> Sure I shall never marry like my sisters,
> To love my father all.   (i. i. 98–103)

The purely sexual associations between Edmund and the two sisters are reversals of the marriage bond, and serve also to show the emptiness of the apparent loyalty of the sisters towards each other, which is so lightly violated for Edmund, even to the point where Goneril poisons Regan. The reversal of Edmund's natural relationship with his father is hammered home too in Cornwall's words to him as they conspire together against Gloucester: 'I will lay trust upon thee; and thou shalt find a dearer father in my love' (iii. v. 23–4).

The process of reversal is a recurrent way of highlighting the moral judgements of this play. Paradox, most prominent in the Fool's songs and epigrams, is a particular kind of truth frequently demonstrated in the play through a process of reversal, as Rosalie Colie has shown.[5] Reversal is one of the most cruel and ironical ways in which the play answers its own questions about the real and the natural: What is a real, or natural, father? a real daughter? real service? real authority? a real king? a real man? Lear's obsession with having given birth to such unnatural daughters of his own flesh, for example, is reversed in the pelican image of his daughters feeding on him, destroying the flesh which gave them life. The sacred relationship between guest and host, revered throughout medieval literature, is reversed with uncompromising cruelty when Cornwall, a guest in Gloucester's castle, blinds Gloucester there. When Cornwall initiates the reversal of their relationship by assuming authority in his host's castle and ordering him to shut the door on Lear, Gloucester sees this as emblematic of the disaster to follow: 'I like not this unnatural dealing. When I desired their leave that I might pity him, they took from me the use of mine own house' (III. iii. 1-3). Like the Elizabethan preachers, Gloucester sees the seeds of chaos in the violation of the natural order of relationship.

Another reversal with strong visual impact points the difference between right and wrong relationship when Lear as father and figure of authority kneels ironically to his children, and then in true humility. When Regan advises Lear to ask Goneril's forgiveness for cursing her and leaving her house, his reaction is one of mocking disbelief:

> Ask her forgiveness?
> Do you but mark how this becomes the house:
> 'Dear daughter, I confess that I am old; [*Kneeling.*
> Age is unnecessary; on my knees I beg
> That you'll vouchsafe me raiment, bed, and food'.
>
> (II. iv. 150-4)

He kneels here as a way of reminding Regan of her unnaturalness in treating him thus, but he kneels in acknowledgement of the way he himself has abused his authority and his relationship with Cordelia, first when he begs her forgiveness (IV. vii. 85), and secondly when he describes their future life as if it were an icon in which he knelt perpetually before his daughter (V. iii. 10-11).

The difference between natural and unnatural relationships can be measured by a comparison of terminology. Cordelia, Kent and the Fool do not ration how much they give, but willingly commit themselves totally. Indeed, the tragedy is set in motion by Cordelia's refusal to measure her love in financial terms and for financial reward. Lear's suffering is deserved to the extent that it is he who introduces the principle of measurement into love, by asking for such declarations from his daughters. Goneril and Regan willingly perjure themselves in the terms he requires, and show Lear the implications of their willingness here in their later propensity towards measurement, when they enumerate his barest needs and the superfluity of his knights. Terence Hawkes has drawn attention to the old homophone of 'love', meaning ' "to appraise, estimate or state the price or value of" ',[6] showing how both senses are present in Cordelia's answer to Lear's demand (I. i. 91-2). It is between these two poles of mean-minded measurement and the generous over-flowing of love that the play balances. Lear learns that the fulfilment of bare physical need is not enough to satisfy a man, and more is needed to confirm his humanity:

> Allow not nature more than nature needs,
> Man's life is cheap as beast's. (II. iv. 265–6)

The themes of need and nature link *King Lear* with contemporary arguments (and their classical sources) on the rightness of society, since necessity and natural instinct are the two most frequently offered origins of society. Society is shown in the play to be both necessary and natural, fulfilling physical and emotional needs. Lear learns after depriving himself of his rightful social position that he is not self-sufficient, 'not ague-proof' (IV. vi. 105). The aspiration towards self-sufficiency, like the solitude it implies, is the mark of the villain and the element of anarchy. Poor Tom's nakedness, the harshness of the elements, the unbalance of Lear's mind, are all reminders of the weakness of the individual, his elementary need of other men. The four on the heath cling together for survival, caring for one another's needs, learning the value of society at its most basic and its most divine. As Thomas à Kempis wrote in the fifteenth century:

> Our lorde hath so ordeyned that we shall lerne echone of other to bear paciently the burden of an other, for in this worlde there is no man without defaute, no man without burden, no man suffycient of hym selfe in wisdome or prudence, & therefore must echone of us helpe to bere the burden of other, echone to comforte other, helpe other, instructe them, & monisshe theym.[7]

But *King Lear* displays its medieval roots even more clearly in its assertion that society is necessary not only for life in terms of survival, but for life in terms of fullness, happiness and spiritual fulfilment. The sense of fellowship is just as important to man's existence as man, as the provision of food and shelter.

The disregard for bonds, the solitary movement inwards towards the self, instead of outwards towards fellowship and the sharing of suffering, is shown to be the source of division and disintegration in society, and of self-division within its individual members. Prophecies of the destruction that will result from this unnaturalness are announced at the beginning of the play, with the resonance of their cumulative occurrence throughout Shakespeare's work from

Richard III on. Gloucester, for example, sees the events of the first Act as emblematic of the times, lamenting that 'we have seen the best of our time: machinations, hollowness, treachery, and all ruinous disorders, follow us disquietly to our graves' (I. ii. 107–9). It is by echoing these words of Gloucester's concerning the various bonds broken, and claiming them to be an astronomical prediction, that Edmund persuades Edgar to flee from his father; although, ironically, despite the fact that they are a fabrication of Edmund's in imitation of Gloucester, they do predict the actual course of events set in motion by the original cracking of bonds:

> . . . unnaturalness between the child and the parent; death, dearth, dissolutions of ancient amities; divisions in state, menaces and maledictions against King and nobles; needless diffidences, banishment of friends, dissipation of cohorts, nuptial breaches, and I know not what. (I. ii. 138–42)

These generalised prophecies are one way in which *King Lear* reaches out to relate its microcosm to society as a whole. This is not a play set, like *Hamlet*, in narrow closets and lobbies, metaphors for the enclosing individual mind which is the real setting of *Hamlet*: it takes place partly in echoing state rooms, but mostly outside walls altogether, on a heath, a cliff, a beach, in harsh, exposed open spaces. Yet the widest, most desolate place is resolutely contained within a social framework. Maynard Mack quotes T. S. Eliot's phrase, ' "the life of significant soil" ',[8] to explain the purpose of Poor Tom's references to villages, farms, and the daily life of a community. The characters of the play themselves represent the entire social spectrum from the king to the beggar, and the vocabulary of social status, bonds, service and nature repeatedly reminds the audience of their social roles and interrelationship. References to the gods set the play in the widest possible context, as does the widening meaning of the word 'nature'. The Fool's comments too imply that what Lear is discovering in the particulars of his own individual life are in fact truisms, repeated in all societies and in all ages. The mirroring of Lear's predicament in Gloucester's is yet another way of illustrating that Lear should not feel isolated and self-bound by his suffering, but should be led through it instead to identify with other men. The play reaches beyond the individual vision which reduced all the world to a purely subjective and relative experience in *Hamlet* to reconstruct a shared vision, a way of escaping from the prison of the self. Those values which are most obviously circumscribed by an individual vision in this play are also most clearly wrong. Right values seem to impose themselves on individuals from outside, from a collective consciousness, rather than to emanate spontaneously from within individuals. For most of the characters, these values are not inherent in their natures; they have to be taught an elementary process of reversal, taught to hold 'vile things precious' (III. ii. 71) and to see that what seemed 'nothing' is in fact everything. Morality ceases to be judged from within the individual perspective, as it is in *Hamlet*, and individual autonomy is rejected so that absolute values may be reinstated. The play affirms the absolute nature of certain social and divine laws, and replaces the relativism which precluded clear-cut moral judgement in *Hamlet* with a simple dialectic between absolutes of good and evil which supersede the individual subjective judgement.

Vision ceases to be a relative concept which draws attention to the differences between individual modes of perception and becomes instead a concept of moral truth to which individuals aspire. The moral judgement is most clearly seen in the way certain individual viewpoints are depicted not as types of vision but quite simply as blindness. Individuals must struggle to transcend their blindness, which is a wrong vision distorted by too much of the self, in order to achieve true vision, through which they participate in a collective perception of truth which enables them to reach beyond the limitations of their individuality. The inclusion of all things external to the self within the introspective mind is not seen as a liberation and expansion of the individual, but as restricting and distorting. The true liberation is the liberation from self, the true expansion the expansion beyond self, which move beyond self-awareness to the recognition of moral absolutes.

The opposition between vision and blindness is symptomatic of the moral and dialectic structure of *King Lear*, already demonstrated in the prevalence of paradox and reversal, didactic devices which employ contrast and suggest moral judgements. This dialectic is unlike the fluidity of *As You Like It* or the Sonnets, unlike the fragmented and highly individualised worlds of *Richard II* and *Hamlet*. The mirror, for example, which had come to stand for the reduction of the world to a purely relative self-image, and the divided nature of such a self and such a world, appears only once in this play (aside from the figurative structural mirrors of parallel and reversal), in a context of such literal simplicity as to act as a corrective to this earlier relativism and fragmentation. It appears literally, as a stage-property, not an image, and is required to arbitrate on the most simple and essential dialectic of all, to which there will always be one right and one wrong answer, the dialectic between life and death. Lear asks for a glass in the final moments of the play with total unconcern for its capacity as image-maker and its associations with self. He only wants to see whether Cordelia's breath will cloud it and prove her to be alive. This is the culminative moment in the play's insistence that there is a right and a wrong, and that all is not an impenetrable morass of reflections within reflections relative to each other. Cordelia is dead, however much Lear, from his individual perspective, may wish or even believe her to be alive. Her death is an unalterable absolute, emblematic of the play's insistence throughout on truth as absolute, not merely subject to the perceiving self.

The language of the play strives in the same way to restore integrity and singleness of meaning to words which have expanded to accommodate so many individual interpretations as to have become almost meaningless. The attempt to restore 'nature' to its medieval universal sense through the moral discrediting of its individual sense is a case in point.[9] Whereas *Hamlet* and the early comedies used irony and pun to break the bond between one word and one meaning, *King Lear* uses paradox not to empty words of meaning, but to restore them to truth, and above all, to social truth. Rosalie Colie has described paradoxy in *Lear* as

> . . . working not to detach one meaning, one idea, one person from another such, as much as to connect them all in a web of significances in which the paradoxes of poverty, blindness, folly, bastardy, barrenness, and the rest are interrelated and interrelate meanings, ideals, and persons in one firm structure.[10]

In striving to reinstate words like the much repeated 'bond', 'truth', 'justice', 'nature', to the semantic simplicity of their medieval status as collectively acknowledged absolutes, the play is simultaneously trying to restore the values they denote as universally acknowledged moral laws. And the return to the simplicity of absolutes in words and values is mirrored in the increasing importance in the play of the most primitive elements of life, the basic essentials of warmth, shelter, company in suffering. The pervasive theme of nakedness, and its linguistic counterpart 'nothing', reflect this same stripping of truth to its barest elements. 'Robes and furr'd gowns' (IV. vi. 165) come to symbolise sophistication, hypocrisy and corruption, while nakedness comes to represent the essential humanity of man. Glibness and ornate speech similarly suggest dissimulation, while plain speaking is the virtue of Cordelia, Kent and the Fool. Yet Lear's initial misunderstanding of Cordelia's words, his wrong response to Kent's intervention and his ability to shut out what the Fool is trying to tell him imply that words are unreliable methods of communication, since they have been twisted out of shape by dissemblers and manipulators. Some of the truest words are spoken in madness and addressed to no one in particular.[11] It is through actions and physical touch that men communicate most deeply and unequivocally in this play. The Fool stays with Lear; Kent returns in disguise to serve him; Cordelia returns with an army to fight for him; Poor Tom leads Gloucester by the arm; all on the heath try to coax one another into the hovel to keep warm; and in Lear's extremity, he asks for a simple physical demonstration of care: 'Pray you undo this button. Thank you, sir' (V. iii. 309).

    In order to reach this simplicity and directness of communication with other men, all that seemed to be self must be discarded. Loss of 'form', which was a divisive experience in *Hamlet*, leads to a deeper reintegration beyond division in *King Lear*. Kent and Edgar have to abandon rank and identity and take on far humbler roles in order to discover what it means to be a man, as opposed to a courtier or a duke's son. They must first disintegrate the old self before they can achieve unity both within and among themselves. Lear too, after casting off the name of king, searches for a sense of identity and finds that his conception of his own significance has been inadequate. No longer respected as king or revered as father, he is forced to examine what it means simply to be a man, and the identity he discovers is one which returns to older values through the older and root sense of the word 'identity', the sense that emphasises what unites men by distinguishing them from the inhuman, and not what divides them by distinguishing them from each other. Kent foreshadows Lear's self-discovery in his earlier acknowledgement of himself as primarily a man. When Lear asks him in his new disguise, 'What art thou?', Kent replies, 'a man, sir' (I. iv. 9–10), anticipating the answer Lear will find when he begins to ask himself the same question. Though social roles are important and should be acknowledged, they can only be observed in the right spirit after men have first understood what unites them in a society at all, what they share on the most primitive level where all become equal.

Like *Hamlet, King Lear* moves towards a definition of manhood. As everywhere in Shakespeare's work, manhood in the sense of humanity, 'kindness' in medieval terminology, is to be distinguished from manhood in the classical sense of 'virtus'. Lear suffers in losing this second kind of manhood when Goneril's cruelty reduces him to tears:

> Life and death! I am asham'd
> That thou hast power to shake my manhood thus.
>
> (I. iv. 296–7)

This is Goneril's definition of manhood, the one she uses to taunt Albany for his inability to perform cruel acts unflinchingly (IV. ii. 68). But this kind of manhood has to be lost if the first is to be attained. The tears which are unmanly and weak according to Goneril's definition are a demonstration of the capacity for suffering and the compassion for the suffering of other men which reveal the common humanity each man shares with other men. Weeping, for others as well as for oneself, is the beginning of the pity that binds men together to form a society. Edgar is twice so overcome with pity, on seeing Lear mad and his father blind, that he can scarcely maintain his disguise; Cordelia weeps for Lear and condemns the pitilessness of her sisters:

> Mine enemy's dog,
> Though he had bit me, should have stood that night
> Against my fire;   (IV. vii. 36–8)

while Edmund proclaims his own depravity in boasting that 'to be tender-minded / Does not become a sword' (V. iii. 32–3), and Regan hers and Edmund's simultaneously in her description of him as 'too good to pity' his father (III. vii. 89).

Mutual compassion breaks down the traditional relationships of social rank into the elementary relationship between man and man on the heath, where the king identifies with the beggar. By entering into the beggar's suffering, the king learns to define man with a new minimum:

Is man no more than this? Consider him well. Thou ow'st the

worm no silk, the beast no hide, the sheep no wool, the cat no perfume. Ha! here's three on's are sophisticated! Thou art the thing itself: unaccommodated man is no more but such a poor, bare, forked animal as thou art. (III. iv. 102-7)

Lear then begins to tear off his clothes in an attempt to become fully identified with Poor Tom, to understand in feeling exactly what essential humanity, 'the thing itself', is like. He recognises the paradox that the least is also the greatest, that man's minimum is also his maximum, since in perceiving the basis of his humanity which unites him with other men a man achieves the fulfilment of his nature. Lear's mind expands beyond his sense of individuality to reach the paradoxical vision which Luther expressed in these words: 'I am a human being; this is certainly a higher title than being a prince, for God did not make a prince; men made him. But that I am a human being is the work of God alone.'[12]

Just as the instinct for community defines man's humanity, so the cultivation of solitude once again defines the inhuman, as in *Richard III*. Goneril and Regan are described in the same imagery as Richard, as beasts, monsters, devils, preying upon themselves and the social order. The self-consuming destructiveness of solitary actions implicit in the linguistic patterns of the Sonnets is made explicit in *King Lear*:

> Humanity must perforce prey on itself,
> Like monsters of the deep.   (IV. ii. 49-50)

Lear's curse on Goneril is remarkably specific, a curse not of injury, misfortune or death, but of sterility. His curse is a recognition of inhumanity, a feeling that Goneril's unnatural rejection of all the bonds that hold society together should have some physical emblem, either in sterility, as in the Sonnets, or in distortions of nature, as in Richard III's deformity or Jaques's venereal sores:

> If she must teem,
> Create her child of spleen, that it may live
> And be a thwart disnatur'd torment to her.   (I. iv. 281-3)

Those who choose to cut themselves off from humanity and remain enclosed within the prison of self are unequivocally condemned.

Hamlet, while not celebrating the alienation of the individual from society, did demonstrate some admiration for the uniqueness, the distinctness of the individual, but *King Lear* celebrates the common bond which lies beyond individual distinctions. It reaches towards 'the mystery of things' (v. iii. 16), an absolute truth which encloses Hamlet's mystery of self and forces *it* to become the merely relative. The mystery of the absolute is one approached not through solitary self-examination, but through fellowship and relationship. Whereas Hamlet, Richard II and the boy of the Sonnets were so self-enclosed that the whole world felt like a prison to them, Lear achieves such an ability to transcend his individual self-awareness that for him a prison can expand to become the whole world if it is shared. In Lear's prison, there is not one alone, but 'two alone', who together can aspire to the expansion of vision denied to the solitary man:

> Come, let's away to prison.
> We two alone will sing like birds i'th'cage;
> When thou dost ask me blessing, I'll kneel down
> And ask of thee forgiveness; so we'll live,
> And pray, and sing, and tell old tales, and laugh
> At gilded butterflies, and hear poor rogues
> Talk of court news; and we'll talk with them too—
> Who loses and who wins; who's in, who's out—
> And take upon's the mystery of things
> As if we were God's spies; and we'll wear out
> In a wall'd prison packs and sects of great ones
> That ebb and flow by th'moon.   (v. iii. 8–19)

10 'Too absolute': *Macbeth, Coriolanus, Timon of Athens*

These late tragedies even more than the rest of Shakespeare's work acknowledge the divided response to the solitary characteristic of Shakespeare's age. They present the solitary man as villain–hero, simultaneously noble in his isolation yet morally condemned for voluntarily seeking it out. The audience must condemn these men for their studied rejection of the social bonds which should define their humanity and yet pity them for their very isolation, perhaps even admire them for the defiance with which they face up to the solitary way they have chosen, a way which necessarily leads to sterility, inhumanity, insignificance and death. Willard Farnham, in *Shakespeare's Tragic Frontier*, has pointed out that, by contrast with Shakespeare's earlier tragedies, there are no villains in these plays.[1] Instead, the central protagonist is inextricably hero and villain at once, even in the same characteristics: 'There is nobility to be found in Timon, Macbeth, Antony, and Coriolanus, but in the main it seems inseparable from their flaws, and an admirer of that nobility may wonder whether he is not admiring the flaws themselves even while he sees that they are flaws.'[2] Primary among the sources of nobility and moral condemnation together is the solitude of these characters, a solitude which is first of all voluntary, but gradually intensifies to a point beyond the individual's control until it destroys him.

Macbeth's tragedy lies in the intensification of his solitude towards this absolute and the consequent sense of utter meaningless-ness that overcomes him after he has finally severed the last bond with society and humanity. The first Act shows the early, voluntary stages of this isolation, in which Macbeth's decision to place self-interest and personal ambition above social duty and responsibility is beginning to take shape. These early scenes separate Macbeth from those around him by contrasting the love and trust felt towards him by his king and commonwealth with his own gradual withdrawal of any reciprocal feeling. The first scene presents no human beings at all, only the witches in a desolate place, emblematic of the movement towards inhumanity and desolation the play will take. The next scene shows the fellowship of men united in battle in the same cause, recounting the battle that has passed. They include Macbeth in their account and by implication in their fellowship, but Macbeth is absent and so cannot confirm or deny his adherence to the common cause. When he does appear in the next scene it is on a heath, in direct confrontation with the witches, but with Banquo for company. The opposition of Banquo and the witches on either side of Macbeth in this scene, like the good and evil angels of a medieval morality play, seems to represent the conflict between the social and the solitary instincts in Macbeth, between his bonds with humanity and the isolating, enclosing world of the inner self and its dark, anti-social desires. Although Banquo sees the witches too, so that it is clear that they are not a simple hallucination of Macbeth's, they do nevertheless bear a strong relation to Macbeth's inner self. Their function is the familiar one of the mirror: they reflect an image of the mind that perceives them. They are not evil in themselves, but an objectification of the evil within Macbeth, as their incapacity to exert any evil influence over Banquo confirms. Already they are evidence that Macbeth's concern with his own thoughts is coming to dominate his perceptions of the external world to the point where it seems a self-image. Their predictions are no novelty to Macbeth, but extensions of half-formulated notions already in his mind, as his guilty start suggests. And their link with his inner self is further implied by the way they immediately transport him into a solitary distraction, making him 'rapt' (I. iii. 57, 142). Even after they have vanished and Ross and Angus have joined the two men, Macbeth remains more in his private mental world than with them. His longest speech in the scene is neither a communication with his friends nor a soliloquy, but an aside, emphasising his ability to cut himself off from other men even in their company, and showing the beginnings of the characteristic self-division of the introspective, solitary man, poised between two worlds, the external and the 'fantastical' (I. iii. 53, 138). Macbeth makes his self-division explicit with unconscious irony when he says:

My thought, whose murder yet is but fantastical,
Shakes so my single state of man

That function is smother'd in surmise,
And nothing is but what is not.   (I. iii. 138–41)

The phrase 'single state of man' simultaneously suggests Macbeth's aspiration towards self-definition in withdrawing from the community[3] and his loss in doing so of 'singleness' in the sense of wholeness, unity of thought and action. As in the Sonnets, 'single' is a word of multiple ironies, like the word 'one' in *Hamlet*, fusing actual isolation with the condemnation of the solitary as fragmented and the longing of the solitary himself for wholeness. Hamlet's longing for wholeness is echoed later in this play when Macbeth makes explicit his desire to be

Whole as the marble, founded as the rock,
As broad and general as the casing air.   (III. iv. 21–3)

It is immediately after Macbeth's musings on his 'single state of man' that the image of ill-fitting clothes which runs through the play is first used of Macbeth. Banquo observes:

New honours come upon him,
Like our strange garments, cleave not to their mould
But with the aid of use,   (I. iii. 144–5)

and the image immediately suggests, with wider implications than Banquo can know, a fundamental disharmony between the inner and the outer man, a suggestion that his public face is not natural to him, but an ill-fitting mask, a flawed and inept performance.

After this scene showing Macbeth alone in company, preoccupied by his inner, fantastical world to the point where he ceases to participate in the external world, there follows a scene which emphasises Macbeth's full consciousness of the duties and bonds he is about to violate. Duncan arrives at Macbeth's castle and is discussing the treachery of the Thane of Cawdor while he awaits Macbeth. His musing on the Thane of Cawdor's powers of dissembling:

There's no art
To find the mind's construction in the face.
He was a gentleman on whom I built
An absolute trust   (I. iv. 11–14)

is the cue for Macbeth to enter, and alerts the audience to the hollowness of Macbeth's words:

> *Dun.* More is thy due than more than all can pay.
> *Macb.* The service and the loyalty I owe,
>   In doing it, pays itself. Your Highness' part
>   Is to receive our duties; and our duties
>   Are to your throne and state children and servants,
>   Which do but what they should by doing everything
>   Safe toward your love and honour.   (21–7)

The words are reliable in as much as they are a true summary of the ideal social order and a direct echo of such medieval statements of the ideal as John of Salisbury's (quoted on p. 120 above), but false in that Macbeth's heart is not in them. His mind is running on how to murder Duncan even as he mouths adherence to his bonds, and the speech simply emphasises the hideousness of the violation to come, since the violator is so aware of the extent of it himself. Before the murder, Macbeth actually summarises the series of bonds between him and Duncan which should forbid such an act:

>   He's here in double trust:
>   First, as I am his kinsman and his subject—
>   Strong both against the deed; then, as his host,
>   Who should against his murderer shut the door,
>   Not bear the knife himself.   (I. vii. 12–16)

And Macbeth is aware too that it is a crime against mankind and against God, an outrage against accepted moral law. Like Richard III, he voluntarily places himself outside the bounds of human and divine law, and is defined as unnatural and inhuman, a beast and a devil, in accordance with the familiar Aristotelian pronouncement. Act II, Scene IV shows the unnaturalness of Macbeth as an individual tainting the external world around him, so that Duncan's horses eat each other, the owl kills the falcon and the sun will not shine. Macbeth's progress from here is towards increasing unnaturalness and inhumanity, which in turn increasingly manifests itself in the commonwealth once he is king, as Richard II's inner disorder manifested itself in his kingdom.

Like its predecessors too, *Macbeth* reaches towards a definition of man. Macbeth at first is closer to the true definition of man's

humanity than his wife, who taunts him with weakness. He sees the
limits beyond which man becomes inhuman clearly at this point:

> I dare do all that may become a man;
> Who dares do more is none,   (i. vii. 46–7)

a vision which Lady Macbeth answers with her own distorted vision
and terminology, reversing the true order:

> What beast was't then
> That made you break this enterprise to me?
> When you durst do it, then you were a man;
> And to be more than what you were, you would
> Be so much more the man.   (47–51)

Initially, the cause of Macbeth's self-division is his need to act
against his own nature in performing the murder of Duncan. He has
to will himself to be unnatural in order to act, has to will, like
Richard III, an opposition between face and heart. The last words of
Act I are an expression of this hardening of the individual will which
betrays the social bonds of trust and duty:

> False face must hide what the false heart doth know.
>   (i. vii. 82)

But, again as with Richard III, this voluntary self-division comes
to seem ironical in the light of the involuntary division that then
invades Macbeth. The first scene of Act II shows Macbeth already
unable to control the division between his public and private
worlds. While he struggles to hide his conscious thoughts, his
unconscious mind transforms the external world into images of
itself. He cannot be certain whether the dagger he sees is a 'dagger of
the mind' (ii. i. 38) or one 'sensible / To feeling as to sight' (36–7). As
Macbeth strives to cultivate an unnatural division between the
inner and the outer worlds, so the two become less distinct for him,
and his inner world distorts his vision of the outer world, which
becomes a prison of the mind. He feels, like Hamlet and Richard II,
'cabin'd, cribb'd, confin'd, bound in / To saucy doubts and fears'
(iii. iv. 24–5). The relativity of perception finds an image in the
equivocation of the witches. What they say is susceptible of so many
interpretations that the words have no absolute meaning, merely a

series of meanings relative to the receptive individual; and in the same way the visual world reflects the beholder and compounds his self-involvement so that he can no longer make judgements which transcend self-interest. As Macbeth turns increasingly against nature, so that 'all that is within him does condemn / Itself for being there' (v. ii. 24–5), his existence becomes increasingly 'self-cover'd' (*Lr.*, iv. ii. 62) and claustrophobic. He cannot escape from the inner world at all, since he has deliberately cut off his commitment to the world about him. He cannot sleep, is tormented by phantoms of conscience even in waking life and becomes progressively more isolated and less human. His initial decision to place his private good before the public good is intensified so that in his concern for individual peace of mind he would subject the community to any amount of suffering:

> But let the frame of things disjoint, both the worlds suffer,
> Ere we will eat our meal in fear and sleep
> In the affliction of these terrible dreams
> That shake us nightly.   (iii. ii. 16–19)

Ironically, this sentiment is voiced after Macbeth has become king, so that the reversal of the right moral order is the more horrifying. As he takes over the responsibility for the commonwealth, the role which should represent the ideal fusion of individual self and body politic, his self-enclosure and self-division are instead confirmed and heightened. This reversal of right order is at its most pronounced in the scene of the feast, the traditional emblem of fellowship and concern for the collective good, where Macbeth is at his most withdrawn and self-obsessed. The events leading up to the feast prepare for its confirmation of Macbeth as social and moral outlaw. Macbeth first mentions it when he urges Banquo to attend as 'our chief guest' (iii. i. 11). Banquo replies in terms which acknowledge the social bond:

> Let your Highness
> Command upon me; to the which my duties
> Are with a most indissoluble tie
> For ever knit.   (15–18)

The reply is doubly ironical: first, Banquo recognises the bond between subject and king which Macbeth is simultaneously plotting to violate by murdering Banquo, and second, Macbeth is to find at the feast that the tie with Banquo is not so easily dissolved as he thought, and is not severed simply by his individual will, but exists even despite the individual refusal to acknowledge it.

Macbeth's isolation is the most prominent feature of the scenes preceding the feast. At the end of the scene where he issues the invitation to Banquo he dismisses all the company, including Lady Macbeth, with this transparent lie:

> to make society
> The sweeter welcome, we will keep ourself
> Till supper-time alone,   (41–3)

and turns to instruct Banquo's murderers, thus confirming his rejection of the bond even with his closest friend. The next scene opens with Lady Macbeth having to request to see her husband through the mediation of a servant. When he comes, she questions him about his withdrawal:

> Why do you keep alone,
> Of sorriest fancies your companions making,
> Using those thoughts which should indeed have died
> With them they think on?   (III. ii. 8–11)

Macbeth's loneliness and the inevitable nature of his solitude now are poignantly clear in this scene, where Macbeth confesses something of his terror and guilt, the 'scorpions' in his mind (36), to another human being. Yet he does not give himself completely, and withholds from Lady Macbeth his plans to murder Banquo, though he feels the need of her company still, if not of her complicity: 'prithee go with me' (56). The request has the simplicity and humanity of Lear's 'Prithee undo this button'.

The banquet scene itself begins with a formal expression of welcome from Macbeth and a statement of purpose:

> Our self will mingle with society
> And play the humble host,   (III. iv. 3–4)

which implies both by its self-consciousness and by the acting metaphor the extent to which Macbeth now finds social intercourse difficult and unnatural. The fact that this mingling with society is

merely a hollow gesture on Macbeth's part is made clear by the fact
that the only speech he utters as he passes round the communal cup
is in asides to Banquo's murderers. His social gestures are mere
ritual dumb-show and his real involvement is in his private schemes.
The inner man reveals himself only in asides, not in direct
communication with his fellow men. Lady Macbeth has to remind
Macbeth of the expressions of community which he has neglected in
his self-absorption:

> My royal lord,
> You do not give the cheer; the feast is sold
> That is not often vouch'd, while 'tis a-making,
> 'Tis given with welcome.   (32–5)

But the inner world intensifies its hold on Macbeth as he acts out the
forms of social expansiveness, taking the grim form of Banquo's
ghost, which, unlike the witches, only Macbeth sees, so that he is
isolated in this respect too. Macbeth's disruption of the feast by his
private hallucinations enacts the threat to social order contained in
the solitary, egotistic impulse of the individual, Lady Macbeth
becomes the spokesman for the condemnation of Macbeth as the
element of chaos in society:

> You have displac'd the mirth, broke the good meeting,
> With most admir'd disorder,   (109–10)

a chaos which is enacted symbolically in the abandonment of the
forms of order as the feast is unceremoniously broken up at Lady
Macbeth's command:

> Stand not upon the order of your going,
> But go at once.   (119–20)

Macbeth, characteristically, is too preoccupied with his own self-
division to show any concern about his divisive effect on society. He
feels, he says, 'strange / Even to the disposition that I owe' (112–13),
realising at the end of this scene that the inevitable advance from
here is towards a hardening inhumanity:

> My strange and self-abuse
> Is the initiate fear that wants hard use.
> We are yet but young in deed.   (142–4)

After this point Macbeth is never again seen in the company of anyone with whom he feels a bond. The only company he seeks out is that of the witches, who show him himself, and whom even his conscious motive in seeking is self-interest. His callousness, remoteness and egocentricity harden, and the descriptions of him reflect this hardening, as does Scotland itself. He is increasingly seen as an inhuman tyrant and fiend, and Scotland is seen as a place where the bonds between man and man are wilfully and violently desecrated:

> Each new morn
> New widows howl, new orphans cry; new sorrows
> Strike heaven on the face, that it resounds
> As if it felt with Scotland and yell'd out
> Like syllable of dolour.   (IV. iii. 4–8)

Macbeth's imposition of his private world on the public world directly reverses the ideal position of the king, whose virtues ought to be primarily social,

> As justice, verity, temp'rance, stableness,
> Bounty, perseverance, mercy, lowliness,
> Devotion, patience, courage, fortitude.   (IV. iii. 92–4)

Instead of ordering his inner life in accordance with the public good, Macbeth devotes himself to his private good to the destruction of the body politic.

But in cutting himself off from social concerns in this way, Macbeth is making his own death more certain than that of his kingdom. This play again affirms society to be the only possible means of survival and fulfilment for the individual, and shows the individual who wilfully severs himself from the social whole to be a meaningless absurdity. Such an individual dies spiritually in cutting himself off from his roots in the body of the commonwealth and has thus nothing to look forward to but the progress of his spiritual sterility towards physical death. Macbeth retains the audience's sympathy because he retains some awareness of the moral absolutes against which he has transgressed, and sees with true vision what he has lost before his death. He does not die in the prison of distorted self-images, but briefly transcends his prison to pass judgement on his own withered incompleteness in his loneliness:

I have liv'd long enough. My way of life
Is fall'n into the sear, the yellow leaf;
And that which should accompany old age,
As honour, love, obedience, troops of friends,
I must not look to have; but in their stead,
Curses not loud but deep, mouth-honour, breath,
Which the poor heart would deny, and dare not.
                                        (v. iii. 22–8)

He recognises the poetic justice of his punishment: he can only hope
to be treated with the same substitution of the forms of sociability for
the thing itself which he has adopted. Like Richard iii, he has a
fleeting vision of himself from society's perspective, accompanied by
a sense of loss for the social comforts he has himself made impossible.

The numbness of inner death forbids him to mourn the death of
Lady Macbeth. Having betrayed the bond between word and truth
in his own dissembling, he is invaded by a sense of the hollowness of
words. More than this, he feels the hollowness and futility of his
whole existence as he recognises his inability to express emotion
even over the severing of this last and most intimate bond. He
himself pronounces the judgement on the meaninglessness of the
isolated part, cut off from any context which would give it meaning.
Having dissembled and betrayed society's trust by cheating it with
mere masks, he has reduced his whole being to the emptiness of a
mask,

              a walking shadow, a poor player
     That struts and frets his hour upon the stage,
     And then is heard no more.   (v. v. 24–6)

Like the player, Macbeth has chosen to reduce himself to a surface
only, one which contradicts his heart, rejecting the wider definition
of the world outside his play, so that his life has sunk to the
meaninglessness of mere solipsism:

                    a tale
     Told by an idiot, full of sound and fury,
     Signifying nothing.   (26–8)

'Signifying nothing' sums up the real deathliness of solitude, the
state in which the individual achieves inhumanity by severing all
bonds with humanity. The severed head which appears on the stage

to announce Macbeth's physical death is mere confirmation of that deathliness.

Coriolanus stands strikingly alone from the first scene of the play, even before he appears. He is described in terms of his opposition to the group, as 'chief enemy to the common people' (I. i. 6–7), a 'very dog to the commonalty' (26–7). As G. R. Hibbard has written in his excellent introduction to the Penguin edition of the play:

> His characteristic stance, whether one sees him in the theatre or in the mind's eye, is that of the solitary figure, the isolated individual, facing a hostile group of other men, driving them back with his sword, cowing them into submission with his scorn or inciting them to fury with his defiance. It is thus that he enters the play, and it is thus that he leaves it.[4]

It is clear that Coriolanus's banishment is the logical consequence of his inward solitariness, and this inward solitariness is itself not a characteristic developed by particular events, but inherent in his nature. As the Second Citizen tells the first, who has accused Coriolanus of pride, 'What he cannot help in his nature you account a vice in him' (I. i. 39–40). Coriolanus's answer to the sentence of banishment imposed on him confirms that it is already more deeply rooted in his will than the mere judgement of men can make it:

> You common cry of curs, whose breath I hate
> As reek o'th'rotten fens, whose loves I prize
> As the dead carcasses of unburied men
> That do corrupt my air—I banish you . . .
>   Despising
> For you the city, thus I turn my back;
> There is a world elsewhere.   (III. iii. 121–4, 135–7)

Shakespeare found in North's translation of Plutarch's *Lives of the Noble Grecians and Romans* this singling out of 'solitarines' as Coriolanus's great fault. North writes:

> Wilfulness is the thing of the world, which a governour of a common wealth for pleasing should shonne, being that which Plato called solitarines. As in the ende, all men that are wilfully geven to a selfe opinion and obstinate minde, and who will never

yeld to others reason, but to their owne; remaine without companie, and forsaken of all men,[5]

and he emphasises throughout his account how aggressively unsociable Coriolanus is, 'churlishe, uncivill, and altogether unfit for any mans conversation'.[6] No matter how much other men admired some of his characteristics, 'they could not be acquainted with him, as one cittizen useth to be with another in the cittie'.[7] It is appropriate, then, that Coriolanus should be banished from the city, since he is clearly unfit for social life. Shakespeare makes his Coriolanus even more aloof, portraying him alone on occasions where Plutarch says he was accompanied. The very word 'alone' dominates the play,[8] both in Coriolanus's own self-descriptions:

O, me alone! Make you a sword of me?   (I. vi. 76)

Alone I fought in your Corioli walls   (I. viii. 8)

I go alone,
Like to a lonely dragon, that his fen
Makes fear'd and talk'd of more than seen   (IV. i. 29–31)

Alone I did it   (V. vi. 117)

and in others' allusions to him:

He is himself alone,
To answer all the city   (I. iv. 52–3)

Know, Rome, that all alone Marcius did fight   (II. i. 153)

Alone he ent'red
The mortal gate of th'city.   (II. ii. 108–9)

As with Richard III and others, the familiar echo of the Geneva Bible in 'himself alone', together with the common people's condemnation of his aspiration towards self-sufficiency, firmly places him outside moral law.

Even the name 'Coriolanus' drives home his singularity and isolation, since it was given to him in recognition of his entering Corioli alone to fight and winning the victory without any help from

other men (in Plutarch he is accompanied by two or three others).
His solitude is not simply incidentally anti-social, but pointedly so,
and hence always presented in a social context. Coriolanus is rarely
alone on stage. His solitude is not the solitude of the introspective,
contemplative disposition, like Hamlet's, but of the egotism and
pride which defines itself by antagonism to society rather than from
within. He is condemned not for being withdrawn and retiring, but
for overvaluing himself. His solitude is visualised as an upward, not
an inward movement:

> *Brutus.*   Caius Marcius was
> A worthy officer i'th'war, but insolent,
> O'ercome with pride, ambitious past all thinking,
> Self-loving—
> *Sicinius*   And affecting one sole throne,
> Without assistance.   (IV. vi. 29–33)

He does not seek the privacy of the inner life, but wants to expand
his own capacity so that he towers alone over all other men,
obliterating their identity in his own monstrous egocentricity.
According to Sicinius, he 'would depopulate the city and / Be every
man himself' (III. i. 264–5). His speech is obsessively dominated by
the first person singular in a way that is unavoidably offensive and
utterly lacking in any capacity for self-criticism. Coriolanus is
certain of his own indispensability, his centrality in the community
he despises:

> I shall be lov'd when I am lack'd,   (IV. i. 15)

and directly provokes his own death at the hands of the Volsces by
boasting of his individual exploits, quite insensitive to or uncon-
cerned by the inappropriateness of this in the circumstances:

> Hail, lords! I am return'd . . .
>   You are to know
> That prosperously I have attempted, and
> With bloody passage led your wars even to
> The gates of Rome . . .
>   like an eagle in a dove-cote, I
> Flutter'd your Volscians in Corioli.
> Alone I did it.   (v. vi. 71, 74–7, 115–17)

The extent to which his world-view is restricted by his pre-occupation with self is clear here, where it prevents him from judging the effect of such insolence in the context. It is neatly suggested too in the early incident where Coriolanus begs a man's life only to find that he has forgotten the man's name (Act 1, Scene ix). An incident that might have been used to play down Coriolanus's self-interest is manipulated instead in such a way that it emphasises after all how peripheral and inconsequential anything beyond himself seems to Coriolanus.[9]

The familiar 'I am' of self-satisfaction echoes through Coriolanus's speech. It is sounded faintly in his first words in the play, in praise of Aufidius:

> And were I anything but what I am,
> I would wish me only he,[10]   (i. i. 229–30)

and is echoed again when he actually meets Aufidius, and strips off his disguise:

> If, Tullus,
> Not yet thou know'st me, and, seeing me, dost not
> Think me for the man I am, necessity
> Commands me name myself.   (iv. v. 54–7)

To Volumnia, he is defiant:

> Would you have me
> False to my nature? Rather say I play
> The man I am,   (iii. ii. 14–16)

and when he leaves his family to go into exile, he is proud:

> While I remain above the ground you shall
> Hear from me still, and never of me aught
> But what is like me formerly.   (iv. i. 51–3)

But the judgement against this stance is pronounced explicitly in the play, even by Volumnia, who tells her son:

> You might have been enough the man you are
> With striving less to be so.   (iii. ii. 19–20)

Her insistence that he is 'too absolute' (III. ii. 39) draws attention to what Coriolanus is trying to do. He is trying to set himself up as the absolute to which all about him is relative, instead of accepting himself as relative and subject to collective absolutes. Again, the word 'singularity' describes both Coriolanus's aspirations and the condemnation of them by society. It is commented on by Sicinius in the first scene of the play (I. i. 276), and implied again in Menenius's taunting of both tribunes when they condemn Coriolanus for being proud:

> *Men.* You blame Marcius for being proud?
> *Bru.* We do it not alone, sir.
> *Men.* I know you can do very little alone; for your helps are many,
> or else your actions would grow wondrous single: your abilities
> are too infant-like for doing much alone.   (II. i. 29–34)

C. T. Onions in *A Shakespeare Glossary* glosses the first instance of 'singularity' as 'peculiar character', and Philip Brockbank in the Arden edition of the play notes some of the glosses of earlier editors, most of which can be subsumed, he says, under the two OED headings of 'Individuality; distinctiveness' and 'distinction . . . due to some superior quality'. It is clear, however, particularly from the second occurrence, where a comparison with Coriolanus is clearly implied, that the word is also closely linked with the idea of solitariness, as it is in the Sonnets and in *Macbeth*, and with the idea of singleness of being of which Coriolanus is so proud. Coriolanus is 'single' in the sense of being 'separate, solitary' (Onions), performing his actions in splendid isolation, without 'helps'; but the condemnation of such isolation and rejection of help is suggested in the sense of 'poor, weak, feeble' (Onions) which Menenius plays on. While he condemns the tribunes for their weakness in being unable to do anything alone, the direct linking of the word 'single' and the sense 'weakness' suggests the opposite of Menenius's intended meaning: that Coriolanus is weakened by cutting himself off from other men. Onions glosses a third meaning of 'single' too, although he does not suggest it is present in *Coriolanus*, the meaning 'single-minded, sincere'. Yet this meaning clearly is implied too in Coriolanus's refusal to act a part, to compromise his absolute nature. His resolve 'not to be other than one thing' (IV. vii. 42) echoes Hamlet's longing 'to say "one"', and the word 'one' suggests the word 'single'. But this same 'singularity' is condemned and admired. Volumnia condemns it as intransigence, while Aufidius's servants are overwhelmed by it: 'He is simply the rarest man i'th'world' (IV. v. 160–1). Hamlet longs for it as an ideal reconcilement of the private with the public self; Coriolanus displays it as the symptom of contempt for society combined with exaggerated reverence towards the self.

This oneness between private and public self, however unattractive, sets Coriolanus apart from the other characters in the play and from the heroes of other plays, who are tormented by their own self-division. Coriolanus, with Hamlet, though from a different perspective, exposes the simplistic idealism of Polonius's maxim that truth to self equals truth to other men. Coriolanus is absolutely and uncompromisingly true to himself, and the outcome is that he is condemned as 'a traitor to the people' (III. iii. 66). His behaviour demonstrates that there are other ways of betrayal besides dissimulation. Hamlet is false to society in that he deliberately cultivates false public masks, puts up false, empty words as a barrier between himself and others, whereas Coriolanus preserves his integrity and truthfulness at the price of fellowship, because he simply does not care what others think of him. Menenius praises this unity of face and heart in Coriolanus: 'His heart's his mouth' (III. i. 257), but the citizens are sensitive to the motive, and recognise it to be a sign of animus against society as unmistakably as dissembling. Coriolanus frames his refusal to ask for the citizens' voices as a refusal to dissemble, but this is no more than the emphasis of terminology. His dislike of dissembling arises out of an over-precious cherishing of his own self, and his refusal to beg for voices less out of a dislike of dissembling than out of pride, an unwillingness to prostitute his treasured person to the rabble and an instinctive withdrawal from anything resembling communication. It is not so much dissembling as words of any kind that he dislikes, whether true or false, since he has no wish to communicate himself to others. Speech is, as Hibbard writes, quoting Ben Jonson:

. . . 'the instrument of society', because without it the intercourse of man and man, which is essential for civilized living, is impossible . . .

Coriolanus's vulnerability to words is connected with his failure as a human being. He cannot converse with other men, for conversation implies reciprocity, and there can be no reciprocity for one who refuses to admit his relationship with others.[11]

Coriolanus's rejection of the social bonds is repeated more explicitly and with clearer condemnation than that of any character in Shakespeare so far discussed. He wilfully severs himself from any relationship with the community, eventually even his family, and aspires to be a whole in himself. Lawrence N. Danson has drawn attention to the prominence of metonymy and synecdoche, linguistic patterns 'of fragmentation and usurpation—of parts representing the whole and of the whole absorbing its parts'[12] in a play which examines the right relationship of part to whole in terms of the individual and society. As Coriolanus increasingly demonstrates his unwillingness to play a part in the communal whole and his aspiration towards self-sufficiency, so the community increasingly rejects him and wants him cut away like a disease, as Sicinius says (III. i. 295). Menenius points out that the cutting off of a diseased limb is mortal (presumably to the limb rather than to the whole body), and the course of the play enacts this truth, showing Coriolanus progressing towards inhumanity and death after he has cut himself off from the living root of the community.

The well-known Aristotelian imagery of god and beast is very prominent in this play.[13] In aspiring to become an absolute which would replace collective absolutes, Coriolanus aspires to be a god, but becomes in effect a beast, a monster, a 'thing'. In fact, the imagery of a god is probably used more often than that of a beast, as a way of underlining the sarcastic contempt his stance provokes. Brutus, for example, condemns him for speaking of the people

> As if you were a god, to punish; not
> A man of their infirmity,   (III. i. 81–2)

and Cominius comments on his status among the Volscians:

> He is their god; he leads them like a thing
> Made by some other deity than Nature,
> That shapes man better.   (IV. vi. 91–3)

His use of the word 'thing' is perhaps even more disturbing in its implications of inhumanity than 'god', and it is often used of Coriolanus. He is described early on as 'a thing of blood' (II. ii. 107), and by the end as 'more than a creeping thing' (v. iv. 13–14), even 'an engine' (v. iv. 19).

In its exploration of what it means to be a man, this play presents a hero who is fully a man in the sense Goneril and Lady Macbeth would define manhood, a shining example of classical *virtus*. And it is by presenting such a man that the play shows such a definition to be inadequate, since Coriolanus idolises his physical prowess to the exclusion of any human concerns. He openly rejects humanity in his own character:

> All bond and privilege of nature, break! . . .
>   I'll never
> Be such a gosling to obey instinct, but stand
> As if a man were author of himself
> And knew no other kin.   (v. iii. 25, 34–7)

Yet ironically this most extreme statement of rejection is made immediately before Coriolanus is forced to acknowledge the bond of nature with his family, which proves him to be human, despite his will to the contrary. Like Richard III and Macbeth, his progress through the play is towards inhumanity and death, but before physical death fixes the inward death which is already almost total, he has a brief experience of natural feeling, a vision of his own humanity. Richard despairs that 'there is no creature loves me'; Macbeth mourns the absence of 'troops of friends'; Coriolanus's eyes 'sweat compassion' (v. iii. 196). But for none of them does this perception of their own distorted vision offer a retreat from the progress away from humanity and towards death. In voluntarily cutting themselves off from their bonds with nature and society they have cut off their own lives at the source and must wither and die. The only movement for the solitary is towards death.

Timon of Athens, perhaps because it appears to be an unfinished play, documents the advancement of the solitary towards death in its starkest outlines. This monolithic singleness of effect may also in part arise out of Plutarch's treatment of Timon, who is not the subject of one of Plutarch's Lives, but merely the subject of two brief digressions. Plutarch gives scarcely any detail about Timon's character: his misanthropy and his retreat into solitude stand out as the only facts about him. There is a simplicity about Shakespeare's Timon too, whose solitude is physical and absolute. He places himself quite literally outside the city walls and does not, like Coriolanus, enter another city, or, as in pastoral, a woodland society. He remains totally outside any community, an outlaw in the most explicit sense, and his only contact with other men is forced on him by the visits others pay him in his solitude.

Subtler forms of solitude exist in the play, of course, besides the physical exile Timon chooses for himself. There is isolation within the city walls as well as outside them, and Timon is isolated in being deluded, the dupe of flatterers, long before he consciously isolates himself. Even the earliest scenes, which depict festive sociability, allow the festivity to be undercut by the solitary figure of Apemantus, who rejects Timon's welcome:

> You shall not make me welcome.
> I come to have thee thrust me out of doors.   (I. ii. 24–5)

Timon's reply:

> Fie, th'art a churl; ye have got a humour there
> Does not become a man; 'tis much to blame   (26–7)

shows him using sociability as a criterion of moral judgement, a judgement which the play turns against Timon.[14] The hectoring tone is reminiscent of contemporary treatises on the relative virtues of solitude and society, which also presented the issue as essentially a moral one.

Apemantus is an uncomfortably obtrusive element of solitude within this society. He is related to both villains and comic outsiders: a cynic, a satirist, a malcontent, a self-defining egotist, a spectator who refuses to participate. His solitude extends even to a stage direction, which describes him as he would wish to be described, in terms of himself alone: 'dropping after all, Apemantus, discontentedly, like himself' (I. ii.). Like Richard III, Jaques, Edmund, and others, he announces his detachment self-consciously ('I come to observe' [I. ii. 33]) and defiantly ('I pray for no man but myself' [61]), and places himself in the tradition of the outsider who tells socially unacceptable truths, like Jaques and the fools. Typically, too, Apemantus is self-divided, and his self-division reveals itself in his simultaneous self-love and self-disgust. He tells Timon of his own self-love (IV. iii. 307–12), but is described by the Poet as loving few things better 'than to abhor himself' (I. i. 63).

In all these respects he anticipates Timon. Unlike Timon, however, he is a solitary by 'nature', as Coriolanus is. Timon, on the other hand, is in the opening scenes of the play Shakespeare's most flamboyantly sociable man. He chooses solitude later as a consequence of a melancholy which is again not natural to him, but a pathological state described by Apemantus as

> a nature but infected,
> A poor unmanly melancholy sprung
> From change of fortune.   (IV. iii. 201–3)

He is afflicted, in the terminology of contemporary medical treatises, not by 'natural' melancholy, but by melancholy 'adust', which causes men 'to bee aliened from the nature of man, and wholy to discarde themselues from all societie, but rather like heremits and olde anchors to liue in grots, caves, and other hidden celles of the earth'.[15] This is of course exactly what Timon does, becoming a solitary in the most primitive sense, a wild man of the woods. For the Elizabethans, Timon was the archetypal solitary, his very name a synonym for solitude. Burton cites 'Timon Misanthropus' as an example of solitude symptomatic of melancholy;[16] Daniel Tuvil, after quoting the familiar Genesis text against solitude, exclaims:

> Hence then with all those *Athenian Timons*, those *Diogenicall Cynickes*, that make their private Mansions, the publike Monuments of their living carkasses, and so retire themselves from all occasions of entercourse, that the very doores of their habitation doe seeme to challenge by way of anticipation, the inscription from their Tombes;[17]

and innumerable others cite him as an example in the same way, consistently condemning his solitude as unnatural, unhealthy, even mortal.[18]

Timon was seen as an *exemplum* of the solitary by the ancients too,[19] and the classical setting of the play, as in *Coriolanus*, evokes the classical debate on solitude very strongly. The Aristotelian dictum is enacted in Timon's descent to bestiality to the point where he even digs for food with his hands. Even more clearly than the action, the speeches of the play echo the classical treatises. Timon's own speech at I. ii. 90 ff. formally discourses on the classical *topoi* of self-sufficiency and whether friends are necessary, even repeating the commonplace so often quoted in the sixteenth century, 'We are born to do benefits' (96–7).

The moral judgement of the play is framed in Christian as well as classical terms, though more ambiguously. The strangers at Act III, Scene ii pass judgement in strongly religious terms, condemning Athenian society and praising Timon, though this is before Timon has withdrawn from society. A late morality play, *Liberality and Prodigality* (performed 1601), may help to suggest how Timon should be judged. In this play, Prodigality seeks company indiscriminately, like Timon, whereas Liberality insists on the necessity for discernment:

> Some men deserve, and yet doe want their due;
> Some men againe, on small deserts do sue.
> It therefore standeth Princes Officers in hand,
> The state of every man rightly to understand,
> That so by ballance of equality,
> Ech man may have his hire accordingly.[20]

It is Flavius, a steward like Liberality, who shows this discernment in *Timon*, and who chides Timon for his vagueness about money, another characteristic he shares with Prodigality, who admits to having lost his money 'in the twinkling of an eye, /Scarce knowing which way' (IV. v. 849–50).

Timon of Athens itself has something of the cast of a morality play and looks back nostalgically, like *Lear*, to medieval times. The minor characters are clearly aligned on the side of virtue or vice, gnomic couplets are scattered throughout and the play is strongly judgemental in character. Like *Lear*, it portrays the 'disruption of feudal morality'[21] and offers self-interest, the substitution of the private for the public good, as the cause. Self-interest takes the form of eagerness for money in this play, and Timon's apostrophe to gold is in the line of the vision of social chaos that reappears in so many of Shakespeare's plays:

> O thou sweet king-killer, and dear divorce
> 'Twixt natural son and sire! thou bright defiler
> Of Hymen's purest bed! . . .   (IV. iii. 379 ff.)

In the first part of the play, Timon stands as an archetype of the closely bonded society of a former age, though, ironically, he stands alone as such, since the society in which he finds himself does not share his ethos. The disintegration of Timon's household clearly parallels the decay of housekeeping so frequently deplored by

Shakespeare's contemporaries as the result of self-interest replacing concern for the public good (see pp. 23–4 above). The word 'keep' is ironically reversed in meaning in the play from keeping open to keeping closed. Timon is forced to shut himself off in his house for refuge where before he voluntarily stayed at home for availability, a reversal similar to the reversals of *King Lear*. As Timon's servant says, in the characteristically proverbial tone of the play:

> And this is all a liberal course allows;
> Who cannot keep his wealth must keep his house.
>
> (III. iii. 40–1)

Timon turns instinctively to the feast, emblem of social concord, as an appropriate setting in which to enact the reversal of his social good will. It recalls the earlier feast at Act I, Scene ii, and reveals in retrospect that it was a violation of all that the feast should symbolise, differing from the second feast only in that its violation was masked by a hypocritical pretence of communal feeling, where the violation of the second is crude and explicit. The ceremonial presentation of gifts and reciprocation of thanks and more gifts at the first feast exposes a devotion to forms at the expense of the spirit. As Timon himself says at the beginning of that feast with unconscious irony:

> ceremony was but devis'd at first
> To set a gloss on faint deeds, hollow welcomes,
> Recanting goodness, sorry ere 'tis shown;
> But where there is true friendship there needs none.
>
> (I. ii. 15–18)

Timon's offering of stones and water in place of food and his hurling of both these at his guests in the second feast violently enacts the reversal which has taken place in Timon's vision, so that where he once saw the first feast as a manifestation of the social nature of man he now sees it in retrospect as a manifestation of the self-love which holds them apart from true community.

Timon is close to *Lear* in its preoccupation with the roots of the true society in nature, need, bonds, the bare elements that define humanity, and in its exposure of a particular civilised society as false. 'Nature', or 'kind', is a consistent standard by which men are judged in these late plays. The individual who erects his own nature into his first principle and tries to define himself in isolation from the context of any society is clearly condemned in the framework of 'nature' in its wider sense, the humanity which all men share. Unlike Lear, and to a lesser extent Macbeth and Coriolanus, Timon never achieves a vision of that wider nature as the highest good. He began with a rather naive and vulnerable form of it, which collapses as soon as it is threatened. He comes to define nature as the lowest common element in man:

> There's nothing level in our cursed natures
> But direct villainy,   (IV. iii. 19–20)

and his use of the plural emphasises the isolation and singleness which undercut such a unity. Men united only by villainy remain men apart.

The bonds that hold society together in this play are exposed with vicious irony as mere extensions of self-interest. The word 'bond' is never applied to kinship here, since Timon is unique among the tragic heroes in having no kin, though he tries to invest friendship and loyalty with equal strength. The second meaning of bond— promise, and by extension, a written security, especially for money—is used to undercut Timon's naive idealism. Only in the first scene does 'bond' retain Timon's idealistic interpretation, first when Timon frees Ventidius by paying his debts, and the messenger quibbles, 'your lordship ever binds him' (I. i. 107), and again when Timon dispenses more money to enable a servant of his to marry a rich girl and justifies his own gift as fulfilling 'a bond in men' (147). But in both instances the word describes an act of Timon's, not any reciprocation of his kindness, and is suspect in any case because money is the focus of both these acts of kindness. In the very next scene Apemantus begins to use the word in the sense of 'promise', notably in a context which questions the validity of men's bonds:

> Grant I may never prove so fond
> To trust man on his oath or bond.   (I. ii. 62–3)

From then on bonds become the pieces of paper that Timon's false friends send him in order to reclaim their money, bonds which confirm the absence of the other kind of bonds. Lucullus makes explicit which kind of bonds Athenian society values more highly when Flaminius asks him to help Timon and he replies: '. . . this is no time to lend money, especially upon bare friendship without security' (III. i. 41–2). The irony is that there can be no security, in the sense of stability, in a society which values financial securities and bonds more highly than friendship.[22] The 'broken bonds' (II. i. 42)[23] returned to Timon mirror the breaking of far deeper bonds in this society.

Legal bonds introduce the principle of measurement already shown to be so destructive to the bonds of nature in *King Lear*. And as in *Lear*, such bonds debase the value of the words in which they are framed. Feste's witty comment in *Twelfth Night*, 'words are very rascals since bonds disgrac'd them' (III. i. 19), sounds the bitter note of truth characteristic of the fool's wit. After leaving the city, Timon tries to reach beyond the fickleness of words to a naked and objective vision, unclouded by individual subjectivity. He chastises the Poet for his words: 'Let it go naked: men may see't the better' (v. i. 65), but he does not really transcend the limitations of words, and remains obsessed by their falseness. His rejection of language: 'Lips, let sour words go by and language end' (v. i. 218) is appropriate to his solitary state. Coriolanus's solitude too was accompanied by a distrust of words, Hamlet's by a deliberate distortion of them. But language does not end for Timon: like Coriolanus, he cannot resist a final expression of his disgust with men, and ends in words, in the abuse of his self-composed epitaph.

The comparison with Coriolanus should not be over-emphasised, however. Timon does not share Coriolanus's genuine recoil from communication. One of the paradoxes of Timon's solitude is his compulsion to communicate it. Roger Baynes, considering Timon as an extreme solitary type, insisted that even he needed someone to tell about his hatred, and this same qualification is suggested in the long scene with Apemantus at Act. IV Scene iii of Shakespeare's play. Both these two are self-professed solitaries, yet Apemantus has sought Timon out and seems unable to leave him, however much he is insulted, and Timon too yields to the need to continue this dialogue of insults even while seeming to dismiss Apemantus. Timon betrays his need of human contact to Alcibiades too in the same breath as he repeats his misanthropy:

> I am Misanthropos, and hate mankind.
> For thy part, I do wish thou wert a dog,
> That I might love thee something.   (IV. iii. 52–4)

Similarly, his inner division between rejection of society and the need for it emerges when Flavius shows loyalty to him:

> How fain would I have hated all mankind!
> And thou redeem'st thyself.   (IV. iii. 499–500)

Even in solitude there is not the singleness, the union of face and heart, that Timon seeks. For him, man is defined by his divided self:

> Each man apart, all single and alone,
> Yet an arch-villain keeps him company.[24]   (v. i. 105–6)

When Alcibiades promises him friendship, Timon replies:

> Promise me friendship, but perform none.
> If thou wilt promise, the gods plague thee, for
> Thou art a man. If thou dost not perform,
> Confound thee, for thou art a man.[25]   (IV. iii. 72–5)

But Timon, unlike Lear, does not achieve a definition of man which transcends the limits of his own subjectivity. His view remains distorted and extremist, as even Apemantus can see: 'The middle of humanity thou never knewest, but the extremity of both ends' (IV. iii. 299–300). Timon's judgement of social man is distorted, echoing society's judgement of the solitary: he sees man in society as first a god, idealised, and then a beast, full of individuals as solitary figuratively as Timon and Apemantus are literally. 'The commonwealth of Athens is become a forest of beasts' (IV. iii. 344–5)— the words are from Apemantus, but the sentiment is shared by Timon.

The very existence of Flavius and Alcibiades, however, proves Timon's definition of man to be inadequate, since it cannot accommodate those who are loyal to their bonds. Timon's distorted conception of humanity mirrors his own alienation from it. He literally moves away from it by placing himself outside the city walls, where his existence becomes increasingly sterile, bestial and inhuman, by refusing to acknowledge his bonds even to those who love him. His solitude is presented in the image of the cave, a stark image of living death in the same tradition as the stream of contemporary imagery of buried torches, covered lamps and living tombs, used by Shakespeare's contemporaries as arguments against solitude.[26] Like Coriolanus and Macbeth, Timon cuts himself off from life in cutting himself off from society, and the perspective of collective absolutes reasserts itself beyond the life of the individual. The solitary, in rejecting the framework of natural absolutes which binds him, destroys not the framework but himself.

Afterword: The Last Plays

It may initially seem strange that a book on solitude should not involve a study of Shakespeare's last plays. The reason for omitting them here is not their irrelevance to the theme of solitude in general terms, but the fact that they seem to demand a different frame of reference from the kinds of solitude analysed in this book. They seem to embody a conviction of the *inevitability* of solitude, which is quite absent from Shakespeare's earlier work and very different from, if not unrelated to, the more specific solitude deliberately cultivated by individuals or imposed on them by particular circumstances. The method of this book has been to concentrate on the solitary figure or figures in a given play and examine their position in relation to the wider frame of reference implied by the play; such a method would be impossible to apply to the last plays, where solitude becomes part of the frame of reference, an unalterable absolute in men's lives.

The Tempest presents this frame of reference at its most explicit and extreme in the image of the island, which contains the whole play. The island, confining all individuals and all action, seems emblematic of a philosophy which stands in direct opposition to Donne's famous pronouncement that 'no man is an island'.[1] In *The Tempest*, every man is an island, unreachable and uncommunicated. The individuals forced together into unwilling retreat do not, as in *As You Like It*, for example, unite to form the characteristic microcosmic society of pastoral. They hold aloof from one another and are ruled by self-centred, not communal, impulses. They have social aims, in a literal sense, but not compatible, since each would be ruler of his own society. Prospero has brought the others together with the aim of restoring the social order which he ruled in Milan before his brother usurped him, but the others have different ideas. Gonzalo has his theory of the ideal commonwealth, Antonio and Sebastian plan to kill Alonso and rule as usurpers respectively in Milan and Naples, Stefano and Trinculo set themselves up as rulers of the island, thinking themselves the only survivors of the wreck,

Ariel longs for freedom from his subjection to Prospero to become master of himself, Caliban longs for the time when he was lord of the island. These are essentially solitary desires: every man longs to be 'Emperor of himselfe',[2] not participant in an order which would subject him to its rules.

It is possible, of course, to see some links between individual characters in this play and the solitary types of earlier plays. Prospero, as governor of a kingdom, is faced with a choice similar to that of Richard II, between his private nature and his public responsibility. He openly admits to having lost his dukedom through his own fault in setting his private desires before the public good. Wholly absorbed by study, he tells Miranda,

> The government I cast upon my brother
> And to my state grew stranger, being transported
> And rapt in secret studies.   (I. ii. 75–7)

Antonio is clearly in the tradition of the villainous egoist who works to destroy the social good, like Edmund or Richard III. His silence in the last scene would seem to indicate that he does not accept Prospero's forgiveness, and chooses to remain solitary even at the end of the play. W. H. Auden's poem, *The Sea and the Mirror*, makes explicit his resemblance to Richard III by giving him as refrain Richard's notorious line, 'I am myself alone'. Caliban's open misanthropy and literal bestiality is not so far removed from Timon's state immediately before his death.

But there is a solitude which runs deeper than these superficial resemblances which, ironically, all share, a natural envelope sealing each individual into his own self and precluding direct communication with others. It is this form of isolation which is more characteristic of the play, and it has been discussed in some detail by Anne Righter in her introduction to the New Penguin edition of the play. She writes:

> Even at its ending *The Tempest* remains compartmentalized. Distinct groups of characters meet at last, but they do not really communicate with one another, and the magician who has ordered these revelations and discoveries is still essentially alone. As in the paintings of Piero della Francesca, the eyes even of people confronting one another directly in conversation do not seem to meet. Instead, the lines of sight stray off at angles. There is a puzzling obliquity of vision. The coming together of all the

characters at the end, a meeting so long expected, only serves to stress the essential lack of relationship, in ways that have an overtone of tragedy.[3]

Words in this play are curiously distanced, even by the self-regarding quality of their beauty. They seem to hang in the air between speaker and audience, spoken sheerly for the indulgence of the aesthetic pleasure they give rather than for the purpose of communication. Prospero's famous speech beginning 'Our revels now are ended' (IV.i. 148ff.) is spoken in the company of Ferdinand and Miranda, but, far from being addressed to them, it is a solitary, meditative utterance, which circles above their heads and breaks off with an apology for its highly individual quality: 'Bear with my weakness; my old brain is troubled' (IV.i. 159). The content of the speech, musing as it does on the illusory nature of the border between dream and reality, draws attention to the state of mind which makes for difficulty in communication. Throughout the play, different characters acknowledge that they feel as though they are in a dream and hence cannot distinguish between the subjective and objective worlds. They feel that the world around them is in fact of their own creating, a dream-world enclosed by the individual mind which fashions and perceives it. Necessarily then, attempts to communicate seem reflexive, mere images of self-communing.

Words confirm the enclosing veils around the individual self by their inwardness. The most intense communication is conveyed through music, and even that is not a communication which relates individuals to one another, but one which reminds them of the boundaries of the inner self by teasing them with its incomprehensibility. They sense it rather than understand it and are impelled by its motion from outside themselves, not the spontaneous initiators of it. Ferdinand tries to explain the indirect, felt nature of this communication beyond words:

> Where should this music be? I'th'air or th'earth?
> It sounds no more; and sure it waits upon
> Some god o'th'island. Sitting on a bank,
> Weeping again the King my father's wreck,
> This music crept by me upon the waters,
> Allaying both their fury and my passion
> With its sweet air; thence have I follow'd it,
> Or it hath drawn me rather. But 'tis gone.
> No, it begins again.   (I. ii. 387–95)

Such 'communication' is essentially a solitary experience, wrapping the self in its own meditations rather than opening it out towards relation. Even Caliban is similarly moved by the sounds of the island in a way that he cannot explain. As he tells Stefano and Trinculo about it (III. ii. 130–8), he becomes paradoxically distanced from them, retreating into the incommunicable intensity of remembered private experience.

Cymbeline, Pericles and *The Winter's Tale* share something of this vision of every man as an island which reaches its limit in *The Tempest*. Posthumus and Imogen, for example, almost bring tragedy on themselves by their inability to communicate with one another. Even their reconciliation has a still-born quality. Posthumus's words on embracing Imogen:

> Hang there like fruit, my soul,
> Till the tree die!   (v. v. 263–4)

with their image of fruit hanging in stillness, unable to achieve the natural dropping motion, suggests very strongly the solitary inner self, unable to achieve the natural motion of reciprocity and communication. Pericles, similarly, seems to have his own necessary isolation forced on him at the moment of closest relationship. Recognising Marina at last as his daughter, he embraces her, and is cut off from her by his sudden perception of music that neither she nor anyone else hears and his subsequent sleep. Leontes is isolated throughout the first part of *The Winter's Tale* by his secret delusions, delusions which he can scarcely make intelligible to the audience,[4] far less to Hermione, who tells him in bewilderment:

> Sir,
> You speak a language that I understand not.
> My life stands in the level of your dreams.   (III. ii. 77–9)

In appealing to the oracle, as a recent critic has argued, 'it is not so much justification Leontes seeks, or the semblance of legality, but the Word which endorses a felt truth and extends beyond itself the validity of a private vision.'[5] In his reconciliation with Hermione too, his perceptions are confused between whether she is cold, unmoving stone, or warm life. Though she moves to embrace him, she is silent, hanging on him as Posthumus on Imogen, unable to speak directly to him. She is not fully alive, Camillo considers, until she speaks:

> She hangs about his neck.
> If she pertain to life, let her speak too.   (v. iii. 112–13)

But when she does speak, she looks away from Leontes towards Perdita, and Leontes looks away from her towards Paulina and Camillo.

At climaxes which in comedy would normally be expected to celebrate the social ethic in confirming union and relationship, these last comedies present an intense, paradoxical experience of isolation in relationship. Despite the unaltered longing for relationship, the continuing sense from Shakespeare's earlier work of the desirability of social fulfilment, these plays seem to despair of the ideal towards which they strive. They portray a natural solitude in man acting as a barrier to inhibit full consummation of the social vision. In reaching out to establish their bonds with those outside them, the characters of these plays merely reaffirm their essentially self-bound and lonely existences. Such involuntary and inescapable solitude is not the proper subject of a book entitled *Shakespeare and the Solitary Man*, which implies the existence of its opposite, the social man, but of an unwritten book with a title of yawning breadth, implying a whole philosophy: *Shakespeare and the Solitude of Man*.

Notes

Where London is the place, or one of the places, of publication, I have simply supplied the date. Otherwise, both place and date of publication are stated.

INTRODUCTION

1. Stefano Guazzo defines these classifications in his *Civile Conversation*, trans. G. Pettie and B. Young, Tudor Translations, 2 vols. (1925), vol. 1, pp. 48–50. See also R. Baynes, *The Praise of Solitarinesse* (1577), p. 85. This threefold classification is basically an elaboration of the distinction between physical and spiritual solitude made by medieval religious writers. Walter Hilton, for example, writing in the fourteenth century, distinguishes between 'bodily enclosing' and 'ghostly enclosing' in *The Scale of Perfection*, ed. E. Underhill (1923), I. i. 2.

2. The changing meaning of the word 'society' in Shakespeare's time sheds some light on the increasing emphasis on the individual as defined from within which characterised the period. Shakespeare always uses 'society' to mean, as Touchstone says, that 'which in the boorish is company' (*AYL*, v. i. 45), but the word was gradually developing a more remote and abstract meaning, a sense which endowed a group of individuals with the impersonality of an institution, so that the group ceased to be thought of as composed primarily of individuals keeping company with each other, and came to be thought of as an abstraction set apart from, almost against, the individual. The OED records its first occurrence in this latter sense, 'the aggregate of persons living together in a more or less ordered community', as 1639, but this date represents the formal embodiment of an attitude which had been hardening since the late sixteenth century.

3. 'The Case of John Webster', *Scrutiny*, 16 (1949), 38–43, p. 42.

4. 'Shakespeare's Politics: with Some Reflections on the Nature of Tradition', *Further Explorations* (1965), 11–32, p. 22.

5. *Shakespeare and Elizabethan Poetry* (1951), p. 100.

6. The seventeenth-century praise of solitude, particularly in lyrical form, has been fully documented by M-S. Røstvig, *The Happy Man*, vol. 1. 1600–1700, 2nd ed., Oslo Studies in English, 2 (Oslo, 1962); M. C. Bradbrook, 'Marvell and the Poetry of Rural Solitude', *RES*, 17 (1941), 37–46; W. L. Ustick, 'Changing Ideals of Aristocratic Character and Conduct in Seventeenth-Century England', *MP*, 30 (1932), 147–66; and H. G. Wright, 'The Theme of Solitude and Retirement in Seventeenth Century Literature', *EA*, 7 (1954), 22–35. Wright discusses the shift in vocabulary on the first page of his article.

7. Notes towards his own 'Life', *Brief Lives*, ed. A. Clark, 2 vols. (Oxford, 1898), vol. I, p. 41.
8. Larry S. Champion, in *Shakespeare's Tragic Perspective* (Athens, Georgia, 1976), sees a similar ambivalence in Shakespeare's times between medieval Christian assumptions about man and secular impulses towards self-assertion, but documents Shakespeare's development rather differently in relation to this conflict. 'The emphasis in the earlier plays is', he says, 'on the individual and the anguish of his internal struggle. In the last plays, Shakespeare broadens the perspective in order to emphasize both the personal and societal nature of such tragedy' (p. 218). Champion is more interested in the individual and society as co-existent but separate sources of tragedy than in the failure of the relationship *between* the two as a single source.

CHAPTER 1

1. *Republic*, VII. 520–1, 540.
2. *Eudemian Ethics*, VII. i. 5. Translations from all classical texts are from the Loeb Classical Library series, unless otherwise stated.
3. *Offices*, I. xliii. 153.
4. *Politics*, I. 2, trans. B. Jowett, *Works*, ed. W. D. Ross, 12 vols. (Oxford, 1928–52), vol. x.
5. *Nicomachean Ethics*, I. vii. 6.
6. *Politics*, I. 2.
7. *Offices*, I. xxxi. 110. Cf. Seneca, *Epistles*, XLI. 9.
8. *Biathanatos*, ed. J. W. Hebel, Facsimile Text Society, I (New York, 1930), I. i. 7. Cf. Walter Ralegh, *The History of the World* (1614), II. iv. 6.
9. M–S. Røstvig's *The Happy Man* discusses the classical origins of seventeenth-century retirement poetry, and M. O'Loughlin's recent book on leisure, *The Garlands of Repose* (1978), based as it is on the distinction between 'civic' and 'retired' leisure, surveys the classical attitudes to retirement with a rather different emphasis, taking into consideration other genres besides the lyric. His last chapter considers two Renaissance writers, Petrarch and Montaigne, in relation to the classical dichotomy which he explores in the major part of his book, and should be compared with Chapters 2 and 3 of this book, which were unfortunately in the finishing stages when Professor O'Loughlin's book appeared.
10. In his book, *Shakespeare's Heroical Histories* (Cambridge, Mass., 1971), David Riggs discusses the influence of the hero of classical histories on Shakespeare's Second Tetralogy.
11. *Hero and Saint* (Oxford, 1971), chs. 1 and 2.
12. See e.g. F. L. Lucas, *Euripides and his Influence* (1924).
13. *Hero and Saint*, p. 169.
14. *Summa Theologica*, literally trans. by Fathers of the English Dominican Province, 20 vols. (1911–25), part II (First Part), Qu. 92, Art. 1. L. C. Knights, in 'Shakespeare's Politics', quotes Aquinas among others to sustain a similar view of medieval ideology. Walter Ullmann, in his most recent book, *Medieval Foundations of Renaissance Humanism* (1977), presents Aquinas as marking the beginning of the Renaissance. The difference, I think, is primarily one of

emphasis and terminology: in other words, in arguing for continuity between medieval and Renaissance thought, one highlights different aspects of that thought from those that might be highlighted in a discussion of the difference, but the two arguments are not mutually exclusive.

15. Trans. J. G. Dawson, quoted in A. P. D'Entrèves, intro., *Selected Political Writings* (Oxford, 1948), pp. xvii–xviii. Professor Knights, surveying medieval emphasis on man's social duty in 'Shakespeare's Politics', omits to mention this crucial exception to the rule, an exception considered morally superior to the rule itself.

16. See C. Butler, *Western Mysticism* (1922).

17. *The Scale of Perfection*, 1. i. 2.

18. *The Letters of Abelard and Heloise*, trans. B. Radice (Harmondsworth, 1974), pp. 190–6.

19. *Ancrene Wisse*, ed. J. R. R. Tolkien, EETS, 249 (1962), pp. 74–6.

20. All quotations from the Bible are taken from an edition of the Geneva Bible published in 1594, an edition which Shakespeare might have used.

21. *The Fire of Love*, trans. C. Wolters (Harmondsworth, 1972), p. 82.

22. A. B. Ferguson discusses these changes at length in *The Articulate Citizen and the English Renaissance* (Durham, N. C., 1965).

23. Harvey, *Works*, ed. A. B. Grosart, 3 vols. (Privately printed, 1884, 1885), vol. 1, pp. 137–8.

24. The phrase occurs regularly among writers on the ideal commonwealth.

25. *A Dialogue between Reginald Pole and Thomas Lupset*, ed. K. M. Burton (1948), p. 46. This work is thought to have been written between 1533 and 1536.

26. *The Boke named The Governour* (1531), ed. H. H. S. Croft, 2 vols. (1880), III. iii. 202.

27. *Dialogue*, p. 31.

28. *Ibid.*, p. 53.

29. Sermon before his Majesty, 19 June 1621, quoted in R. H. Tawney, *Religion and the Rise of Capitalism*, 2nd ed. (Harmondsworth, 1938, rpt 1975), p. 140. My debt to Tawney should be evident throughout Part One. It will be obvious, however, that I have not attempted to consider the influence of the Reformation on attitudes to solitude, since the subject is too large to treat in brief without distortion.

30. A. Romei, *The Courtiers Academie*, trans. I. K[epers] (n.pl., n.d.), pp. 47–8, quoted in full on p. 85 below. Romei does not acknowledge that this passage is lifted from Pico's *Oration on the Dignity of Man*.

31. *Dialogue*, p. 24. See also R. Kelso, *The Doctrine of the English Gentleman in the Sixteenth Century* (Urbana, 1929), on the difference between the English and Italian codes of courtesy.

32. *Giovanni Pico della Mirandola: His Life . . . Also Three of his Letters . . .*, ed. J. M. Rigg (1890), p. 40.

33. *Complete Works*, ed. E. Surtz and J. H. Hexter (1963–), vol. IV, p. 57.

34. J. H. Hexter has made a study of the relation between the composition of *Utopia* and the events of More's life in *More's 'Utopia'* (Princeton, 1952).

35. See e.g. F. Caspari. *Humanism and the Social Order in Tudor England* (Chicago, 1954), pp. 277–8, n. 30.

36. *Dialogue*, p. 61.

37. *Governour*, 1. i. 3–4.

CHAPTER 2

1. Professor O'Loughlin's account of 'Petrarch and the Life of Solitude' (*The Garlands of Repose*, pp. 224–34) is in some respects close to mine, but differs primarily in its reading of Petrarch's *De Vita Solitaria* as 'unmistakably Christian contemplative' in character (p. 227). The *Vita* seems to me more striking in its deviations from the tradition of Christian contemplative writings than in any adherence to it.
2. *Familiarum Rerum Libri*, IV. i. 154, *Edizione Nazionale delle Opere di Francesco Petrarca*, vols. x–xiii, ed. V. Rossi [and U. Bosco] (Florence, 1933–62). All subsequent quotations concerning the ascent of Mount Ventoux are taken from the same letter. Since Petrarch's ideas are so crucial to the book, and since there is no complete modern edition of his works either in the original or in English translation (the Edizione Nazionale is incomplete), I quote through-out in both Latin and English.
3. *Letters from Petrarch*, sel. and trans. M. Bishop (1966), p. 46.
4. *Familiarum*, XVII. v. 248.
5. *Letters*, trans. Bishop, p. 150. The two treatises are *De Vita Solitaria* and *De Otio Religioso*. Petrarch's letters, particularly the letters from Vaucluse, constantly exhibit his preoccupation with solitude. See also *Petrarch at Vaucluse: Letters in Verse and Prose*, trans. E. H. Wilkins (Chicago, 1958).
6. *De Vita Solitaria* (hereafter cited as *Vita*), *Prose*, ed. G. Martelloti *et al.* (Milan and Naples, 1955), II. xv. 588.
7. *The Life of Solitude*, trans. J. Zeitlin (Urbana, 1924), p. 315.
8. See J. E. Seigel, ' "Civic Humanism" or Ciceronian Rhetoric: The Culture of Petrarch and Bruni', *Past and Present*, 34 (1966), 3–48.
9. *Vita*, p. 290.
10. Zeitlin, p. 100.
11. *Familiarum*, XI. xii. 351.
12. *Letters*, trans. Bishop, p. 106.
13. *Vita*, I. vi. 354.
14. Zeitlin, p. 148.
15. *Vita*, I. iii. 328–30.
16. Zeitlin, p. 131.
17. *Vita*, I. i. 296.
18. Zeitlin, p. 105.
19. *The Advancement of Learning*, *Works*, ed. J. Spedding, R. L. Ellis and D. D. Heath, 14 vols. (1857–74), vol. III, p. 276.
20. See N. Nelson, 'Individualism as a Criterion of the Renaissance', *JEGP*, 32 (1933), 316–34, on the importance of 'singularity' in a definition of the elusive 'individualism', so often said to characterise the period.
21. *Eropaideia: The Institution of a Young Noble Man* (Oxford, 1607), p. 63. Cf. *The Essays of Montaigne*, trans. J. Florio (1603), Tudor Translations, 3 vols. (1892), I. xx. 174.
22. *The Book of the Courtier*, trans. T. Hoby (1561), Tudor Translations (1900), p. 59.
23. T. Lodge, *Wits Miserie, and the Worlds Madnesse: Discovering the Devils Incarnat of this Age* (1596), p. 17.
24. J. Webster, *The White Devil*, ed. J. R. Brown, 2nd ed. (1966), III. iii. 75–81.

25. *The Scourge of Villanie* (1598), *Poems*, ed. A. Davenport (Liverpool, 1961).

26. *Works*, ed. A. B. Grosart, 12 vols. (Privately printed, 1881–3), Vol. XII, p. 172.

27. *Leycesters Common-wealth* (n. pl., 1641), pp. 161–2.

28. *Life in the English Country House* (1978), p. 54.

29. *Ibid.*, p. 108.

30. His treatise, *Publick Employment and an Active Life prefer'd to Solitude . . .* (1667), is an anomaly in his writing. Most of the time, notably in personal documents such as his letters and diary, he displays a pronounced preference for solitude. He even planned at one time to found a society in retirement dedicated to study, meditation and prayer, with cells for each individual. See his letter to the Hon. Robert Boyle, 3 September 1659, in *Diary and Correspondence*, ed. W. Bray (1818, rpt 1906), pp. 590–2.

31. *Diary*, ed. E. S. de Beer, 2nd ed. (1959), 17 May 1643.

32. *Ibid.*, 10 September 1677. The growth of privacy in family life during the sixteenth and early seventeenth centuries is discussed in some detail in M. James, *Family, Lineage, and Civil Society* (Oxford, 1974).

33. *The Steele Glas* (1576), *Complete Works*, ed. J. W. Cunliffe, 2 vols. (Cambridge, 1907, 1910), vol. II, p. 154.

34. *The Duchess of Malfi*, ed. J. R. Brown (1964), II. i. 85–6.

35. *Skialetheia*, Shakespeare Association Facsimiles, 2 (1931), Satyra Quinta, sig. D6^r.

36. *The Overburian Characters*, ed. W. J. Paylor, The Percy Reprints, 13 (Oxford, 1936), pp. 21–2.

37. *Microcosmography*, ed. P. Bliss, rpt with adds. by S. T. Irwin (1897), pp. 82–3.

38. *Picturae Loquentes*, Luttrell Reprints, 1 (Oxford, 1946), pp. 29–30.

39. *Biathanatos*, I. ii. 2.

40. *Ibid.*

41. E. Spenser, *The Faerie Queene* (1596), VI. ix. 30, *Poetical Works*, ed. J. C. Smith and E. de Selincourt (1912, rpt 1969).

42. *Devotions upon Emergent Occasions* (1624), ed. W. H. Draper [1926], IV. 23.

43. For fuller discussion see T. Greene, 'The Flexibility of the Self in Renaissance Literature', *The Disciplines of Criticism*, ed. P. Demetz, T. Greene and L. Nelson Jun. (1968), pp. 241–64.

44. *New Organon*, I. xlii, *Works*, vol. IV, p. 54.

45. *Works*, vol. VI, p. 705.

46. *Two Sermons on these words of Peter the Apostle: Honour all men: Love brotherly felowship*, pp. 24–5. Cf. the much more famous passage from the *Homilie against disobedience and wilfull rebellion* (1571), *Certaine Sermons appointed by the Queenes Majestie . . .* (rpt 1582), sig. Aaa2^r.

47. *Complete Works*, ed. A. Feuillerat, 4 vols. (Cambridge, 1912–26), vol. I, p. 90.

48. *Scourge of Villanie*, Presentation.

49. R. V. Holdsworth, in his introduction to *'Every Man in his Humour' and 'The Alchemist': A Casebook* (1978), makes this point. Citing yet another statement of self-definition, Fitzdottrel's 'I will be what I am' (in Jonson's *The Devil is an Ass* (1616)), he goes on to compare a series of such defiantly self-contained characters with Jonson's idea of 'the poet as isolated hero, "high, and aloofe", his own law-maker, "Who (like a circle bounded in it selfe) / Contaynes as much, as man in fulnesse may"' (p. 20).

50. *Essays*, II. viii. 66. Ernst Cassirer has discussed the novelty of this view in 'Some

Remarks on the Question of the Originality of the Renaissance', *JHI*, 4 (1943), 49–56; and Joan Webber, in a detailed study of seventeenth-century English prose, *The Eloquent 'I'* (Madison, 1968), has emphasised the increasing importance of the notion of style as a mirror of self in this period.

51. *Observations upon Religio Medici*, Scolar Press Facsimile (Menston, 1973), p. 53.
52. *Loose Fantasies*, ed. V. Gabrieli, Temi e Testi, 14 (Rome, 1968), p. 173.
53. *Ibid.*, p. 283.
54. *Autobiography* (begun *c.* 1643), ed. S. Lee, 2nd ed. (1906), p. 132.
55. *Life* (written 1609), *Reliquiae Bodleianae* [ed. T. Hearne] (1703), p. 13.
56. *A True Relation of the Birth, Breeding, and Life, of Margaret Cavendish, Duchess of Newcastle* (1656), ed. E. Brydges (Kent, 1814), p. 27.
57. 'Of Solitude', *Essays Plays and Sundry Verses*, ed. A. R. Waller (Cambridge, 1906), p. 394. Cowley's essays were first published in 1668.
58. *Pierce Penniless his Supplication to the Devil* (1592), '*The Unfortunate Traveller*' and *other Works*, ed. J. B. Steane (Harmondsworth, 1972), p. 64.

CHAPTER 3

1. G. Mackenzie, *A Moral Essay, Preferring Solitude to Publick Employment . . .*, (1665, rpt 1685), p. 50.
2. *Discourse on Civill Life*, pp. 20–1.
3. The phrase is attributed to Scipio by Cato, and would have been most familiar to Renaissance readers through Cicero's quotation of it in his *Offices* (III. i. 1). Petrarch quotes it in his *De Vita Solitaria* (pp. 586–8) and Browne in his *Religio Medici* (II. x), to mention only two.
4. *Vita*, II. xv. 588.
5. *The Praise of Solitarinesse*, p. 4.
6. *The Prayse of Private Life* (composed between 1605 and 1612), I. xxiii, *The Letters and Epigrams of Sir John Harington together with 'The Prayse of Private Life'*, ed. N. E. McClure (Philadelphia, 1930), p. 348.
7. *Cyvile and uncyvile Life*, sig. Aiiiᵛ.
8. *Essays*, II. i. 7.
9. *Ibid.*, III. xi. 288.
10. *The Anatomy of Melancholy*, ed. H. Jackson, 3 vols. (1932), vol. I, p. 11.
11. *Religio Medici*, I. xxxiv, *Works*, ed. G. Keynes, new ed., 4 vols. (1964), vol. I, p. 45. Other critics have noted the prevalence of division and duality in the period. See e.g. M. B. Smith, *Dualities in Shakespeare* (Toronto, 1966); F. J. Warnke, *Versions of Baroque* (1972); and, more specifically on the divided response to melancholy and hence to solitude, L. Babb, *The Elizabethan Malady*, (East Lansing, 1951) and B. G. Lyons, *Voices of Melancholy* (1971).
12. *Advancement of Learning*, p. 420.
13. *Ibid.*
14. *Godfrey of Bulloigne, or The Recoverie of Jerusalem*, trans. E. Fairefax (1600), sigs. A2ᵛ–A3ʳ. I cite this edition because Tasso's exposition is not usually printed as a preface to modern editions of his poem.
15. Letter to Ralegh, *Poetical Works*, p. 407.
16. 'The First Anniversary' (1611), *Complete English Poems*, ed. A. J. Smith (Harmondsworth, 1971), p. 276.

17. I am indebted in my references to sermons to J. W. Blench, *Preaching in England in the late Fifteenth and Sixteenth Centuries* (Oxford, 1964).
18. Bacon, *Advancement of Learning*, p. 430.
19. *Machiavelli's 'The Prince': An Elizabethan Translation*, ed. H. Craig (Chapel Hill, 1944), pp. 66–7. Future reference in the text is to this edition. Hardin Craig does not suggest a precise dating for this translation.
20. *Courtier*, trans. Hoby, p. 125. Future reference in the text is to this edition.
21. *The Civilization of the Renaissance in Italy*, trans. S. G. C. Middlemore (1929), p. 382.
22. W. Caxton (trans.), *The Book of the Ordre of Chyvalry* (1484), ed. A. T. P. Byles, EETS, 168 (1926), p. 113.
23. *The Scholemaster* (1570), ed. E. Arber, English Reprints (1870), p. 66. For an account of the changing attitudes to Machiavelli in England between 1500 and 1700, see F. Raab, *The English Face of Machiavelli* (1964).
24. S. Sheppard, 'On Mr Webster's Most Excellent Tragedy Called the White Devill', *Epigrams Theological, Philosophical, and Romantick* (1651), pp. 133–4, quoted in R. V. Holdsworth, intro., '*The White Devil' and 'The Duchess of Malfi': A Casebook* (1975), p. 13.
25. See e.g. R. Withington, 'The Development of the "Vice"', *Essays in Memory of Barrett Wendell by his Assistants* (Cambridge, Mass., 1926), 153–67 and B. Spivack, *Shakespeare and the Allegory of Evil* (1958).
26. Cf. also D. Bush, 'The Isolation of the Renaissance Hero', *Reason and the Imagination*, ed. J. A. Mazzeo (1962), pp. 57–69.
27. *The Conspiracy and Tragedy of Charles Duke of Byron* (1608), III. iii. 140–5, *Plays and Poems*, ed. T. M. Parrott, 2 vols (1910, 1914), vol. I.
28. Wolfgang Clemen, in *English Tragedy before Shakespeare*, trans. T. S. Dorsch (1961), has examined the development of soliloquy and its implications in more detail.
29. *Tragedy and Melodrama* (Seattle, 1968), p. 13.

CHAPTER 4

1. This division has been discussed by many critics. See e.g. W. B. Toole, 'The Motif of Psychic Division in *Richard III*', *ShS*, 27 (1974), 21–32, or Ralph Berry's excellent discussion of the centrality of the idea of *playing* in Richard's world in *The Shakespearean Metaphor* (1978), ch. 1.
2. The first statement specifically echoes the Geneva version, which Shakespeare knew. The Bishops' Bible and the Great Bible both read simply 'alone', not 'himself alone'. E. A. J. Honigmann links *Richard III* with Marlowe's cult of 'witty profanity' in his introduction to the New Penguin edition (Harmondsworth, 1968), p. 22, but does not include either of these echoes among the examples of Scriptural parody he cites from the play.
3. Michael Goldman, in *Shakespeare and the Energies of Drama* (Princeton, 1972), has noted the importance of the '"himself himself" figure' (p. 24) in relation to what he describes as 'the theme of the "unsounded self"', surely the great motif in early Shakespeare' (p. 18).
4. Spenser, *Faerie Queene*, v. xii. 1.
5. The terminology is also reminiscent of Matthew 10:21: 'And the brother shall

betray the brother to death, and the father the sonne, and the children shall rise against their parents, and shal cause them to die'. My attention was first drawn to this parallel by Harold Skulsky's noting of the similarity between this text and the prophetic speeches in *Lear* (see pp. 127–8 below) in his article '*King Lear* and the Meaning of Chaos', *SQ*, 17 (1966), 3–17, p. 13.

6. Emrys Jones has also described the gradual subjection of Richard to the moral framework beyond him in *The Origins of Shakespeare* (Oxford, 1977), pp. 203–4.

CHAPTER 5

1. I am indebted to E. H. Kantorowicz's invaluable discussion of this theory in *The King's Two Bodies* (Princeton, 1957) throughout the chapter.
2. J. F. Danby, *Shakespeare's Doctrine of Nature* (1949), p. 170. Danby's whole discussion of the meaning of kingship for Shakespeare and his contemporaries is relevant here.
3. 'Person and Office in Shakespeare's Plays', Annual Shakespeare Lecture of the British Academy (1970), pp. 11–12.
4. *Basilicon Doron*, Scolar Press Facsimile (Menston, 1969), I. 4.
5. E. Plowden, *Commentaries or Reports* (1816), p. 213, quoted in Kantorowicz, *The King's Two Bodies*, p. 9.
6. James I warned his son that 'a King is as one set on a skaffold, whose smallest actions & gestures al the people gazingly do behold' (*Basilicon Doron*, III. 121). Anne Righter, in *Shakespeare and the Idea of the Play* (1962, rpt Harmondsworth, 1967), devotes a chapter to 'The Player King'.
7. C. E. Montague, reviewing a performance of *Richard II* in *The Manchester Guardian* (4 December 1899), quoted in *Richard II: A Casebook*, ed. N. Brooke (1973), p. 67.
8. *Advancement of Learning*, pp. 394–5.
9. *Ham.*, III. ii. 366–72; *Ant.*, IV. xiv. 2–11.
10. Peter Ure, in 'The Looking Glass of Richard II', *PQ*, 34 (1955), 219–24, assembles many of the traditional contexts and interpretations of the mirror, and E. R. Curtius, in *European Literature and the Latin Middle Ages*, trans. W. R. Trask (1953), p. 336, has a valuable footnote on the classical treatment of the image. Louise Vinge's *The Narcissus Theme in Western European Literature up to the Early 19th Century*, trans. R. Dewsnap *et al.* (Lund, 1967), contains a full account of traditional interpretations of the Narcissus myth, also relevant here.
11. See Ure, 'Looking Glass', p. 223.
12. *Devotions upon Emergent Occasions*, ed. W. H. Draper [1926], VIII. 50–1.
13. On the garden's associations with enclosure, see S. Stewart, *The Enclosed Garden* (1966); and on its associations with the commonwealth, see Peter Ure's introduction to the Arden edition of the play (1966, rpt 1970), p. lii.
14. 'Person and Office', p. 16.
15. *Essays*, III. ii. 21–2. Robert Ellrodt discusses the similarity between Shakespeare's and Montaigne's interest in self-consciousness in 'Self-Consciousness in Montaigne and Shakespeare', *ShS*, 28 (1975), 37–50.
16. Peter Ure argues, in a note on this speech in the Arden edition, that Richard 'is referring to the prison and not to the human microcosm', but it seems to me that the fusion of all outside space with the little world of the inward self is

crucial to an understanding of Richard; the confusion in language between prison and individual mirrors the confusion in Richard's judgement, which refers all external space back to his own individual inner space.

CHAPTER 6

1. For full discussion of how the first six sonnets form a group, see W. M. Nowottny, 'Formal Elements in Shakespeare's Sonnets: Sonnets I–VI', *EIC*, 2 (1952), 76–84. Since there is no space here to engage in arguments concerning the order of the sequence, I can do no more than simply state the assumption underlying this chapter, that the usual order is more or less correct.
2. *Shakespeare's Dramatic Meditations* (Oxford, 1976), p. 16.
3. *The Wisdom of the Ancients*, p. 705.
4. Cf. pp. 27–8 above.
5. The influence of Platonic terminology, in which 'shadows' describe the manifestations of this world as a pale imitation of ideal reality, is evident here. Arthur Golding too, in his translation of the Narcissus myth from Ovid's *Metamorphoses*, uses 'shadow' to translate words which suggest the insubstantiality of the reflection and its distance from the thing itself.
6. The phrase is taken from Louise Vinge's *The Narcissus Theme*, p. 183.
7. Sir Thomas Smith, for example, writes: 'So in the house and familie is the first and most naturall (but private) apparance of one of the best kindes of a common wealth, that is called Aristocratia where a few and the best doe governe' (*De Republica Anglorum*, ed. L. Alston and F. W. Maitland (Cambridge, 1906), p. 22).
8. *The History of the World*, Preface, sig. Alᵛ.
9. *Ibid.*
10. *Courtiers Academie*, pp. 47–8.
11. *Shakespeare's Dramatic Meditations*, p. 101.
12. The glass was also used as an image of self-consciousness in love in twelfth-century lyrics. See F. Goldin, *The Mirror of Narcissus in the Courtly Love Lyric* (Ithaca, N.Y., 1967).

CHAPTER 7

1. *Arcadia*, pp. 13–14.
2. See R. Williams, *The Country and the City* (1973), Appendix.
3. 'The Oaten Flute', *The Oaten Flute* (Cambridge, Mass., 1975), pp. 21–2. Since writing this chapter I have discovered another very interesting article which judges Jaques in the context of pastoral solitude, Judy Z. Kronenfeld's 'Shakespeare's Jaques and the Pastoral Cult of Solitude', *TSLL*, 18 (1976–7), 451–73.
4. 'Pastoral and Soledad', *The Oaten Flute*, p. 182.
5. 'The Oaten Flute', *ibid.*, p. 22.
6. 'Pastoral Love', *ibid.*, p. 22. Judy Kronenfeld's essay implies that the mirroring of the individual mind in the landscape is peculiar to the melancholy, solitary individual, but this is too restrictive, I think. Jaques is not the only character in the play to experience the forest as a self-image, and the link is conventional

outside Shakespeare too. Spenser, for example, shows Meliboee upbraiding Calidore for thinking that the pastoral life is a matter of place and explaining to him that place is irrelevant, but bears the imprint of the perceiving mind (*Faerie Queene*, VI. ix. esp. 29–31).

7. 'Golden world', or 'golden age' were terms habitually used to refer to the ideal world of innocence which pastoral tried to recreate, an ideal most familiar to Renaissance readers via Ovid's account of the golden age at the beginning of Book I of his *Metamorphoses*. Sidney extends the notion of the golden world to describe the idealisation of all art, not only pastoral, and writes in *The Defence of Poesie*: 'Nature never set foorth the earth in so rich Tapistry as diverse Poets have done . . . her world is brasen, the Poets only deliver a golden' (*Works*, vol. III, p. 8).

8. Judy Kronenfeld takes the ending of the play to reveal 'a change of heart' (p. 468) in Jaques, 'who now turns from his amoral and backbiting pursuit of the cult of solitude to the *vita contemplativa*' (p. 469). The ending, she believes, shows Jaques beginning 'to comprehend the proper uses of solitude' (p. 470).

9. *The Cankered Muse* (1959), pp. 116–17.

10. See note 6 above.

11. More serious implications of the parallel between the debate element in the play and the contemporary debates on solitude are discussed by Judy Kronenfeld, pp. 467–8.

12. Rosalind says Orlando is not a conventional lover at III. ii. 346ff. But see below, p. 100.

13. My attention was first drawn to this point by K. T. van den Berg ('Theatrical Fiction and the Reality of Love in *As You Like It*', *PMLA*, 90 (1975), 885–93), who argues further that Rosalind in her male disguise actually resembles Orlando (p. 890). Cf. opp. Judy Kronenfeld's description of Orlando as 'the man of action, ultimately too sensible to be captured by that pastoral idleness that sentimentally exploits the reflection of one's ego in the landscape' (p. 459).

14. D. Young, *The Heart's Forest* (1972), p. 50.

15. Van den Berg, p. 886.

16. *Explorations 3* (1976), p. 119.

17. *Complete English Poems*, p. 193.

18. *Essays*, III. ii. 21.

19. *The Malcontent*, I. ii. 146, *Plays*, ed. H. H. Wood, vols. I, III (1934, 1939), vol. I.

20. R. Ellis, 'The Fool in Shakespeare: A Study in Alienation', *CritQ*, 10 (1968), 245–68, p. 260.

21. T. F. Connolly, in 'Shakespeare and the Double Man', *SQ*, I (1950), 30–5, has written on the idea of two characters completing a single self.

22. For a different interpretation of this scene, which emphasises the condemnation of Jaques as its primary focus, see Judy Kronenfeld's article, pp. 458–9.

CHAPTER 8

1. I refer only to the works so far studied in this book. It is possible to find examples of solitude treated with some degree of sympathy before *Hamlet*, notably perhaps in the figure of Brutus in *Julius Caesar*.

2. *Essays*, III. x. 257.

3. 'The First Anniversary', *Complete English Poems*, p. 276.
4. W. L. Godshalk, *Patterning in Shakespearean Drama* (The Hague and Paris, 1973), p. 178.
5. *Works*, vol. vi, pp. 431–2. Cf. Trilling's very different reading of this crucial passage, in *Sincerity and Authenticity*, pp. 3–4.
6. *The Shakespearean Metaphor*, p. 62.
7. *Fools of Time* (Toronto, 1967), p. 29.
8. Terence Eagleton has also written on this theme in *Shakespeare and Society* (1967). His argument on *Hamlet* is similar to the argument here: 'Society may indeed be seen as false', he writes, 'its offered definitions as distorting, but it is still the only available way for a man to confirm himself as real, to objectify and know himself in public action' (p. 62).
9. *Fools of Time*, p. 99.
10. Cf. Spenser, quoted on p. 27 above. Florio's Montaigne is even closer in phrasing: 'Life in it selfe is neither good nor evill: it is the place of good or evill, according as you prepare it for them' (*Essays*, i. xix. 86).
11. See P. L. McNamara, 'Hamlet's Mirrors', *Ariel*, 4 (1973), 3–16.
12. David Pirie also quotes T. S. Eliot's famous phrase in his article '*Hamlet* without the Prince', *CritQ*, 14 (1972), 293–314, p. 301.
13. As T. McAlindon has written, 'In *Hamlet*, the problem of lost and false identity is virtually identified with the loss or abuse of "form" ' (*Shakespeare and Decorum* [1973], p. 44).
14. In the sense of 'consciousness'. See C. T. Onions, *A Shakespeare Glossary*, 2nd ed. (Oxford, 1941, rpt 1977). This reading is adopted by most modern editors.
15. See T. Hawkes, *Shakespeare's Talking Animals* (1973), for further discussion of the conflict between language and communication in *Hamlet*.
16. *Essays*, ii. xviii. 402–3.
17. B. McElroy, *Shakespeare's Mature Tragedies* (Princeton, 1973), p. 23.

CHAPTER 9

1. *Shakespeare: Seven Tragedies* (1976), p. 108.
2. M. Mack, '*King Lear' in Our Time* (1966), p. 110.
3. *The Statesman's Book of John of Salisbury*, trans. J. Dickinson (New York, 1927), vi. xx. 243–4.
4. [L. Ducci] *Ars Aulica* [trans. E. Blount] (1607), p. 52.
5. *Paradoxia Epidemica* (Princeton, 1966), p. 461.
6. ' "Love" in *King Lear'*, *RES*, n.s., 10 (1959), 178–81, p. 178.
7. *The Earliest English Translation of the First Three Books of the 'De Imitatione Christi'* . . . , ed. J. K. Ingram, EETS, ES, 63 (1893), i. xvi. 165.
8. '*King Lear' in Our Time*, p. 101.
9. See Danby, *Shakespeare's Doctrine of Nature*, for a full and indispensable discussion of the meanings of the word 'nature' explored in the play.
10. *Shakespeare's Living Art* (Princeton, 1974), p. 352.
11. Further discussion of language here is rendered superfluous by Winifred Nowottny's brilliant essay, 'Some Aspects of the Style of *King Lear*', *ShS*, 13 (1960), 49–57.
12. Sermon on Creed, *What Luther Says: An Anthology*, ed. E. M. Plass, 3 vols. (St

Louis, 1959), vol. II, p. 2733, quoted in R. M. Frye, *Shakespeare and Christian Doctrine* (1963), p. 199.

CHAPTER 10

1. *Shakespeare's Tragic Frontier* (Berkeley and Los Angeles, 1950), p. 8.
2. *Ibid.*, pp. 9–10. Although I have chosen not to consider *Antony and Cleopatra* here, I have discussed the solitude of Antony compared with that of Coriolanus and Timon in my article, ' "Solitarinesse": Shakespeare and Plutarch', *JEGP*, vol. 78, no. 3 (July, 1979).
3. The word 'state' was changing in meaning in Shakespeare's time, its political sense only just emerging. See the brief discussions of this semantic development in J. H. Hexter, *The Vision of Politics on the Eve of the Reformation* (1973), p. 152ff., and W. G. Zeeveld, *The Temper of Shakespeare's Thought*, (1974), pp. 82–3.
4. *Coriolanus* (Harmondsworth, 1967, rpt 1976), p. 8. Criticism of this play has always centred on Coriolanus's solitariness. The citing of examples would be purely arbitrary.
5. *Lives*, trans. T. North, Tudor Translations, 6 vols. (1895–6), vol. II, p. 160.
6. *Ibid.*, vol. II, p. 144.
7. *Ibid.*
8. According to the Harvard Concordance, it occurs fourteen times, a frequency increased only in the Sonnets.
9. M. W. MacCallum, in *Shakespeare's Roman Plays and Their Background* (1910), interprets the incident favourably for Coriolanus (p. 581).
10. As Ralph Berry points out (*The Shakespearean Metaphor*, p. 89), this wish is paralleled by Aufidius:

> I would I were a Roman; for I cannot,
> Being a Volsce, be that I am. (I. x. 4–5)

11. *Coriolanus*, p. 33.
12. 'Metonymy and *Coriolanus*', *PQ*, 52 (1973), 30–42, p. 30.
13. It has been studied in detail by F. N. Lees, 'Coriolanus, Aristotle, and Bacon', *RES*, n.s., 1 (1950), 114–25.
14. Interestingly, the first recorded instance in the OED of 'sociable' in the sense of seeking out and being affable in company, rather than merely being 'naturally inclined or disposed to be in company with others of the same species' shows the same judgemental tone and moral indignation. It is taken from Harvey's Letter-book, in 1573: 'This is he that accuseth me of not being sociable, himself so sociable as you se.' This confirms that sociability was seen as a moral quality by which a man might be judged in Shakespeare's time.
15. T. W[alkington], *The Opticke Glasse of Humors* (1607), p. 68.
16. *Anatomy of Melancholy*, Part. 1, III. i. 2 vol. 1, p. 396.
17. *Vade Mecum*, 3rd ed. (1638), pp. 40–1.
18. J. W. Draper lists some of these in 'The Theme of *Timon of Athens*', *MLR*, 29 (1934), 20–34.
19. See G. Bullough (ed.), *Narrative and Dramatic Sources of Shakespeare*, 8 vols. (1966–75), vol. VI.

20. *The Contention between Liberality and Prodigality*, The Malone Society Reprints (1913), III, vi. 715–20.
21. The phrase is the title of an article by E. C. Pettet: '*Timon of Athens*: The Disruption of Feudal Morality', *RES*, 23 (1947), 321–36.
22. The same pun is used to make a similar point by the Duke in *Measure for Measure*: 'There is scarce truth enough alive to make societies secure; but security enough to make fellowships accurst. Much upon this riddle runs the wisdom of the world' (III. ii. 213–15).
23. Alexander prints 'date-broke bonds', but J. C. Maxwell (New Cambridge), H. J. Oliver (Arden) and G. R. Hibbard (New Penguin) all follow the Folio in printing 'broken bonds'.
24. It is interesting to compare Shakespeare with a possible source at this point. If Shakespeare knew Lucian's *Timon*, he deliberately altered the sense here to turn a commonplace into yet another assertion of the inevitability and destructiveness of self-division in the solitary man. Since Shakespeare would have known Lucian, if at all, in translation, I quote first from Erasmus's Latin, and then from an English translation of 1634. Lucian's Timon affirms: at vita solitaria, qualis est lupis: ununsquisque sibi amicus Timon: caeteros omnes hostes, & insidiarum machinatores' (*Timon, seu Misantropus, Querela Pacis* (Basle, [1517]), p. 306), or, according to Francis Hickes's translation: 'I will eate alone as wolves do, and have but one friend in the world to beare mee companie, and that shall be Timon: all others shall be enemies and traitors' (*Timon, or the Manhater, Certain Select Dialogues*, Watergate Library, 3 [1926], p. 161).
25. I follow G. R. Hibbard's reading here (though line numbers refer to Alexander's text). This reading appears to me to make better sense in the context of the command immediately preceding at line 71 and accords better with the general theme of promise and non-performance emphasised throughout the play.
26. Shakespeare himself uses the image of the torch to condemn solitariness in *Measure for Measure*:

> Heaven doth with us as we with torches do,
> Not light them for themselves; for if our virtues
> Did not go forth of us, 'twere all alike
> As if we had them not.   (I. i. 33–6)

AFTERWORD

1. *Devotions*, XVII. 108.
2. See p. 27 above.
3. *The Tempest* (Harmondsworth, 1968, rpt 1971), p. 40.
4. It is possible that the notorious difficulty of Leontes's early speech at I. ii. 138ff., for example, is intentionally incomprehensible in order to make the point that Leontes is walled in in a secret, incommunicable world. Cf. A. F. Bellette's argument in 'Truth and Utterance in *The Winter's Tale*', *ShS*, 31 (1978), 65–75.
5. Bellette, 'Truth and Utterance', p. 69.

Index of Proper Names

Where two identical endnote numbers occur on the same page they are distinguished by the chapter number following in square brackets. Endnotes referring to the play which is the subject of the same chapter are not indexed. References to characters in plays are indexed under the title of the play, not the name of the character. The first entries under Shakespeare index Part One only.